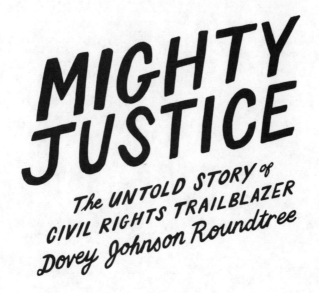

MIGHTY JUSTICE

The UNTOLD STORY of
CIVIL RIGHTS TRAILBLAZER
Dovey Johnson Roundtree

MIGHTY JUSTICE

The UNTOLD STORY of CIVIL RIGHTS TRAILBLAZER Dovey Johnson Roundtree

DOVEY JOHNSON ROUNDTREE and **KATIE McCABE**

ADAPTED BY JABARI ASIM

ROARING BROOK PRESS
New York

Text copyright © 2020 by Katie McCabe and the Dovey
Johnson Roundtree Educational Trust
Published by Roaring Brook Press
Roaring Brook Press is a division of Holtzbrinck Publishing
Holdings Limited Partnership
120 Broadway, New York, NY 10271
mackids.com

Library of Congress Control Number: 2020916485

ISBN 978-1-250-22900-7

Our books may be purchased in bulk for promotional, educational, or business use.
Please contact your local bookseller or the Macmillan Corporate and
Premium Sales Department at (800) 221-7945 ext. 5442 or by email
at MacmillanSpecialMarkets@macmillan.com.

First Young Reader's edition, 2020
Book design by Elizabeth Clark

Adapted from the book *Justice Older Than the Law: The Life of Dovey Johnson
Roundtree* by Dovey Johnson Roundtree and Katie McCabe, originally published
by the University Press of Mississippi in 2009 and reissued as *Mighty Justice: My
Life in Civil Rights* by Algonquin Books of Chapel Hill, a division of
Workman Publishing, in 2019.

Printed in the United States of America by
LSC Communications, Harrisonburg, Virginia

1 3 5 7 9 10 8 6 4 2

To Charlene, Bruce, and James

MIGHTY JUSTICE

The UNTOLD STORY of CIVIL RIGHTS TRAILBLAZER Dovey Johnson Roundtree

CHAPTER 1

WALKING UNAFRAID

"Dovey! Dovey Mae Johnson, do you hear me calling you?" Her grandmother's voice, soft yet strong, landed in Dovey's ears like music. She hurried toward the sound.

"Yes, ma'am?"

Rachel Graham stood in front of the mirror, adjusting her hat. "I'm going downtown," she said. "I want you to go with me."

Dovey could hardly believe what she'd heard. She had often dreamed of accompanying her grandmother on errands, and now it was finally happening. Dovey was only six, but she felt like a big girl at last.

She was so excited that she nearly forgot to hold her grand-mother's hand as they made their way up the block. Soon the streetcar arrived, clanging and squeaking. The minute the trolley doors swung open, Dovey clambered up the steps and plopped into the first empty seat she spotted, right behind the driver. She sat straight up in her seat and grinned at Grandma.

But the driver was not smiling. He whirled around in his seat, and his face turned red. "Get that pickaninny out of here!" he yelled. "You know she can't sit in that seat." He had used a word that white people often used when referring to Black children. Dovey had never heard it before, but she knew it was an insult. She had no idea she'd chosen a seat reserved for white passengers. In a flash, Grandma Rachel pulled the cord to stop the trolley, yanking Dovey down the steps as soon as it screeched to a halt. She led Dovey into town without saying a word, ignoring every trolley that passed their way. Dovey had to run to keep up with Grandma, who quickened her pace with each block. Trolley after trolley passed, but Grandma never stopped. To Dovey, the journey was the longest mile she'd ever walked. More troubling than the driver's stinging remark was Grandma Rachel's silence.

Little had changed in Charlotte, North Carolina, since Dovey was born there in 1914. Like most cities in the United States, it was divided by race. White people lived on one side of Charlotte; anyone who wasn't white lived on the other. Black people were confined to neighborhoods in the Second

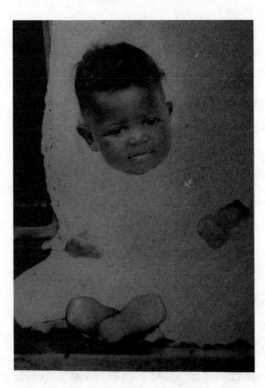

Dovey Johnson, July 1914, on the occasion of her baptism at Charlotte's East Stonewall AME Zion Church by her maternal grandfather, Rev. Clyde L. Graham.

Ward, including Brooklyn, where the Johnsons lived, and Blue Heaven, an even poorer community beside it.

After the end of slavery in 1865, North Carolina and other southern states established Black Codes, laws designed to block African Americans' access to all their country had to offer. The codes enforced a system of racial separation in every place where people gathered, including stores, restaurants, buses, and sidewalks. Whites confined Blacks to underfunded schools, denied them the right to vote, prevented them from testifying in court, discouraged them from owning land, and forced them to endure life as second-class citizens.

Violence and cruelty were used to make sure Black people followed the rules. An organization called the Ku Klux Klan, founded after the Civil War to terrorize former slaves, rose up with renewed fierceness during the years of Dovey's childhood. In southern cities such as Charlotte, mobs of Klansmen, dressed in white hoods, frequently gathered to terrorize Black people with public executions called lynchings. By the time Dovey was born, southern whites had lynched thousands of African Americans. Any Black people who challenged racial segregation risked not only their lives but also the lives of their families and neighbors. The formal name for the system was segregation, but in those days most folks called it Jim Crow.

At the age of six, Dovey had looked Jim Crow full in the face for the first time, and it had hurt. For the rest of her life, she would remember the sting of the trolley car driver's insult and the hatred in his voice. But there was something far greater than the shame of that moment that she took with her, something fierce and proud in the words that Grandma Rachel spoke to her and the family that evening.

Dovey:

> *It wasn't until after dinner that she finally spoke about the trolley car. Just as she did every night, she lit the kerosene lamp in the sitting room and cleared a space for my grandfather to open the old family Bible. Then she disappeared into the kitchen to take*

her cinnamon and butter pastries—"stickies," she called them—from the oven. It seemed to me that she was gone an unusually long time.

"Something bad happened to Dovey Mae today," she said.

I felt my cheeks grow hot, and I looked down.

"The mean old conductor man on the trolley car called her a bad name."

No one spoke. In the lamplight, I looked up into Grandma's face, and I knew she was almost as angry as she'd been that morning.

"I want to tell you all something," she said. She looked around the table at each of us. Her gaze rested last on me.

"Now hear me, and hear me good," she said. "My chillun is as good as anybody."

Only from a distance of years is it possible for me to fathom the courage required for my grandmother to pick herself up from such humiliation and speak those words. I believe, now, that in the long moment when she vanished into the kitchen, Grandma was crying. Certainly she was reaching down into her heart's core, for she was wrestling with the greatest curse of segregation: the horror of having to watch one's own children and grandchildren face its degradation.

In the course of my life, I have heard Black people say they got used to the pain of segregation, eventually. I weep for the numbness of mind and the brokenness of spirit that motivates statements like that. Let me say here for all time that never for one moment of my life under Jim Crow did I grow accustomed to being excluded, banned, pushed aside, reduced. I was never to take a back seat on a trolley or bus, drink the rusty water that trickled from the "Colored" fountains, smell the garbage in the back-alley entrance to segregated movie theaters, or scratch myself on the rough toilet paper in the Black restrooms but that I felt personally violated. And I know, having seen the look on Grandma's face that night, that she felt the same way. Powerful as she was, she could not protect me from the thing she most hated.

But she could arm me. And arm me she did, with words that lifted me up and made me forever proud: "My chillun is as good as anybody."

In Dovey's mind, no one was as wise or as brave as Grandma Rachel. Even before Dovey saw how fiercely her grandmother defied the ugliness of segregation, she had felt the force of Grandma Rachel's strength. In the darkest time of Dovey's young life, in the days and weeks after the sudden death of her father, James, Grandma had risen up to heal the family and enfold it in love.

Dovey had been not quite five when her father died of influenza, a deadly disease that was sweeping the country. For the rest of her life, she would remember that as a time of darkness. Lela, Dovey's mother, seemed to be swallowed whole with sadness. Before her husband's death, she had been playful and active, quick to laugh or jump hopscotch with her daughters. After his passing, she fell silent,

Dovey Johnson's father, James Eliot Johnson, a printer at the AME Zion Church publishing house and a devoted Sunday School teacher.

stopped grooming herself, and refused to eat. Dovey missed the sound of her mother's voice and the way light seemed to ripple through her long, wavy locks when she ran a comb through them. Lela's heartache terrified Dovey and her sisters, Beatrice, Eunice, and little Rachel. It must have frightened their grandmother as well, but she didn't let her fear stop her. She stepped in and took the children under her wing, moving them and her grieving daughter from their home into the parsonage she shared with her husband, Rev. Clyde L. Graham.

All that long winter of 1919, Grandma Rachel battled the forces of sadness that threatened to envelop the household. She rose early, said her prayers, rolled up her sleeves, and went at the day's work with all she had. As the morning darkness gave way to faint hints of dawn, she filled the house with the scents of cinnamon pastries, roasted sweet potatoes, and beans simmering alongside ham hocks in a great iron pot. She used every ingredient, every time-tested recipe, as a weapon against the gloom.

Dovey Johnson's maternal grandmother, Rachel Bryant Graham, circa 1915. Dovey identified her as the single most important influence in her life.

Lela's sorrow was stubborn, pressing her to her bed like a heavy weight. But Grandma Rachel worked to root it out. For weeks, she moved between the kitchen and the bedroom with tea, treats, and encouraging words. Back and forth she went until Lela began to show signs of life. Finally, while stringing beans with her mother one day on the back porch, Lela threw back her head and laughed. She chortled loudly, as if tossing away the melancholy that had clung to her so tightly.

Dovey was in the kitchen with her sisters when she heard the sound. So was Grandpa Clyde, peering intently at his Bible. They all paused to take in the sweet melody of Lela's laughter. Then, one by one, they all joined in.

That day marked a turning point for the family, one that couldn't have happened without Grandma Rachel's fierce and unflagging love. But Dovey wasn't entirely surprised. By then, she had developed a bottomless faith in her grandmother.

Though Rachel Graham stood only five feet tall, she was a giant in her community.

She was the first lady of her husband's church, an active member of the National Association for the Advancement of Colored People (NAACP), and a kindly mentor to all who sought her wise counsel.

Dovey spent many hours at her grandmother's side, marveling at her seemingly endless talents. Dovey especially loved autumn mornings when Grandma made soap in a huge cauldron darkened from years of exposure to an open flame. While a crowd of admiring neighbors looked on, Rachel filled the pot with fat drippings and Red Devil lye, built a fire beneath it, and stirred. And stirred some more while the neighbor women giggled and traded secrets. Tirelessly, patiently, Grandma tended the foaming mixture until suddenly, like magic, it began to take shape. After it cooled, she cut the freshly molded soap into cakes that bleached clothes so white they dazzled the eye.

In Dovey's mind, there was nothing that Grandma Rachel couldn't do, no mystery she couldn't untangle, no problem she couldn't solve. She knew how to follow the flight of birds to the thickets where the ripest berries hid. She knew how to calm a colicky baby, soothe a troubled neighbor, and conjure healing potions from gypsum weed and a handful of herbs. She performed those wonders so swiftly and skillfully that Dovey never could sort out just how Grandma Rachel performed her magic, no matter how closely she watched.

In the evenings, though, Rachel slowed down and tended her own wounds. After filling a metal pan with hot water and laying out clean towels and the ointment she'd made with turpentine and mutton tallow, she sat down and took off her stockings, revealing her battered, twisted feet. They were scarred and so swollen that they didn't seem to fit her small body.

Dovey was frightened the first time she saw them, before the chafes and bruises disappeared beneath the steaming water. In time, though, she learned to wait until her grandmother relaxed, the lines in her face softening as the steam rose. Then Dovey rubbed Grandma Rachel's feet, gently massaging the tender places on her soles and between her toes. The balm's pungent fumes made Dovey wrinkle her nose as the concoction began to do its work. She cherished this time alone with her grandmother, who was so busy during the daytime hours taking care of the family that she barely paused.

Years passed before Grandma Rachel took Dovey aside and explained how her feet had been injured. "I was just thirteen," she told her granddaughter, "and he was meanin' to bother me." Rachel was talking about the overseer on the farm in Henrietta, North Carolina, where her father had worked. Dovey listened, horrified as her grandmother relived the terrible moment. "I ran and fought every way I knew how. And I hurt him. Then he grabbed hold o' me and he stomped, hard as he could, on my feet—to keep me from runnin' for good, he told me.

"But I kept on runnin'. Wasn't nothin' to do but fight him. He wasn't goin' to have his way with me."

Although it hurt Dovey to learn the truth about her grandmother's injury, the knowledge strengthened her as well. Her grandmother had saved herself by fighting, and she had never stopped. Dovey had seen Grandma Rachel's strength the day she yanked her from the trolley car and walked the mile to town rather than remain in the presence of the hateful trolley car driver. She had seen Grandma's courage again on the dreadful summer night when a horde of Klansmen had ridden on horseback through their neighborhood. Grandma had swept Dovey and her mother and sisters under the kitchen table, and then she'd paced in the darkness, broom in hand, letting the family know that she would protect them at any cost. Yes, Grandma Rachel was a fighter, and it thrilled Dovey to realize that the same blood flowed through her veins.

As Dovey grew older, she learned more about the toughness and bravery her grandmother had shown again and again. As a young woman, she'd picked herself up when her first husband was killed by the Ku Klux Klan. Grandma had moved forward after that terrible loss and rebuilt her life when she married Clyde.

Grandpa Clyde was an extraordinary person in his own right. As pastor of East Stonewall African Methodist Episcopal Zion Church, he was a leader in a revered denomination that traced its roots to missionary work in the South before the Civil War. From the time Dovey was small, she understood that the AME Zion Church stood for great ideas like freedom, uplift through education, and the belief that a better day was coming for Black people. She stood tall on Sunday mornings as she and her mother and sisters took their places alongside Grandpa and Grandma to lead the procession through the neighborhood to the door of East Stonewall.

Grandpa was more than just a preacher and a scholar of Scripture. To support his family, he supplemented the food donations that ministers received as payment from their congregations by running a small convenience store during the week. He greeted customers and made change while considering the ideas that would form his sermon.

In addition to taking in laundry, Grandma Rachel labored all week to help prepare for Sunday service. She washed the linens for the altar and kneaded and shaped the dough that would become golden morsels of Communion bread. Every day, the entire household hummed with activity, and delectable scents rose from the pans and kettles in the kitchen and filled the air.

Through all her years spent cooking, sewing, guiding, and praying, Rachel had done all she could to shield her family from the ugliness of racial prejudice. She challenged them at every turn to lift themselves, holding up the example of the most powerful and accomplished Black woman in America, Mary McLeod Bethune, who had risen from poverty to found a Florida women's college and advise presidents. Stories of Dr. Bethune filled the church newspapers from which Grandpa

Civil rights activist and college president Mary McLeod Bethune, circa 1920s.

Clyde read, and people in the neighborhood spoke in awed tones of the way she'd faced down the Klan when they'd tried to burn her college. She'd started that college, they said, in a tiny cabin with five pupils and used packing crates for desks and elderberry juice for ink. Dovey never knew exactly how her grandmother, with only a third-grade education, became friends with the illustrious Dr. Bethune. But from the time Dovey was ten or eleven years old, she recalled Grandma entertaining the great woman in the parsonage parlor. For Dovey and her three sisters, Mary McLeod Bethune came to symbolize all that was possible for African American women. So Grandma said, and so Dovey believed: If Bethune, one of seventeen children born to slaves in South Carolina, could rise to such heights, anything was possible. The way forward for Black children, Grandma Rachel believed, was education.

Grandpa Clyde preached this every Sunday at East Stonewall AME Zion, and he lived this creed every day of the week. At night he spread books across the kitchen table, studying until he was too tired to continue. For his granddaughters, he saved his coins and invested in *The Book of Knowledge*, purchasing the entire set of encyclopedias, one volume at a time.

Dovey waited eagerly each month for the newest installment to arrive. She loved the red leather covers and all the wonders the books contained, including maps of distant lands and colorful illustrations of creatures great and small.

But as a little girl, Dovey was full of energy and mischief, and when she started at Myers Street elementary school, she had a hard time learning to sit still and pay attention. Visits to the family's home by her teachers and scoldings from Grandma Rachel eventually led her to settle down. When Dovey was in eighth grade, a teacher named Edythe Wimbish took her firmly in hand, assigning her tasks in the school library and demanding in her gentle way that

Myers Street School, the all-Black elementary school Dovey Johnson attended in Charlotte, North Carolina.

The campus of Spelman College, Atlanta, Georgia, which Dovey Johnson attended from 1934 to 1938.

Dovey buckle down. Miss Wimbish, who hailed from an illustrious Atlanta family, called upon Dovey's mother and grandparents often, emphasizing Dovey's potential for higher education. She often spoke in glowing terms about Spelman College in Atlanta, Georgia, which she called the finest institution in America for young Black women. To Dovey's family, Miss Wimbish's word was gold. Spelman College became a dream for Dovey from eighth grade onward, and she threw herself into her studies.

But in 1929, her sophomore year in high school, hard times hit the nation with the force of a hurricane. The stock market fell, collapsing the economy and disrupting the lives of Americans everywhere. Banks failed, leaving their customers with empty pockets and bare cupboards. Hungry families formed long lines to wait for free handouts of bread. Businesses closed, and shuttered storefronts blighted the streets of US cities. The effects of the Great Depression, as the economic downturn came to be known, touched the lives of almost every family, including Dovey's.

The white businessmen who had brought shirts for Rachel to launder stopped coming. Grandpa Clyde's store went out of business. Depressed, he began to drink. When his habit grew until he could no longer properly operate East Stonewall, his bishop removed him from his position, and the family had to leave the parsonage. Dovey's grandfather moved from church to church, but eventually none would take him on. Food and money were scarce, but Rachel drew her brood close, and together they kept on fighting.

Although shadows lengthened across Charlotte, the clouds occasionally parted to reveal glints of light. The wealthiest families still needed people to prepare their meals, wash and fold their laundry, scrub their floors, and polish their silverware until it shone. They needed help, and they were willing to pay for it.

Dovey's mother accepted a job with one such family, and Dovey sometimes pitched in to assist Lela on weekends. Against great odds, the family kept food on the table—and hope in their hearts. Dovey was proud of the way her mother had emerged from her grief. Lela earned the bulk of the household income by day and attended school at night, studying dressmaking and tailoring. Eventually she became so skilled that a demand for her services grew despite the effects of the Depression, when nearly half of all Black people were out of work.

Growing up, Dovey had always looked up to her mother as the leader and star vocalist of the choir at East Stonewall, where her alto voice soared above the pews while she accompanied herself on the piano. As Dovey approached adulthood, she began to notice that beneath her mother's sweet temperament lay a great store of ambition. When Lela spoke of her daughters' futures, she proclaimed that they were destined for great things. Nothing would stop them from blossoming into phenomenal women—not poverty, not injustice, not the limited vision of those who couldn't see them as anything but second-class citizens.

Dovey and her sisters came to view the world as their mother did—as a place of opportunity for those who worked hard. Beaming with pride, the younger girls joined their mother and grandparents in bidding farewell to their oldest sister, Bea, as she left for Winston-Salem Teachers College. Soon it would be Dovey's turn to graduate, and she had her heart set on the college Edythe Wimbish had first mentioned when Dovey was in eighth grade: Spelman.

Dovey had been enchanted by Miss Wimbish's description of a place where young women—young *Black* women— could read and study to their hearts' delight. After graduating from Spelman, they would be well equipped to go out into the world as doctors, educators, and community leaders.

Dovey sighed, imagining herself strolling amid sun-splashed greenery, schoolbooks in hand. Her mother's dreamy expression told her that Lela was picturing a similar scene. The future as Miss Wimbish had depicted it made perfect sense. After all, Dovey was as good as anybody. Surely she would be good enough for Spelman.

Grandma Rachel was less enthusiastic. She could still remember when riotous whites had torn through Atlanta in 1906, chasing down Black people and killing them in the streets. Twenty-five years later, she feared it was still Klan country. Besides the threat of imminent peril, there was the cost. At Winston-Salem Teachers College, the state paid the tuition. No such help was available at Spelman, where the yearly tuition was $75, and room and board was $225. Studying there for four years would cost a student $1,200, or eight times the cost of Bea's school.

Lela and Dovey would not be deterred. Through all their struggles, hadn't Dovey's elders reminded her of the importance of doing well in school? Hadn't they told her again and again that college would provide a route to a better life? Lela didn't know what path would lead her brilliant girl to Spelman's gates, but she was determined to find it.

By the time Dovey graduated from high school, no solution had emerged. July passed with no answer. August came and still nothing. Just when Dovey had begun to despair that she might never see Atlanta, Lela came home with promising

Dovey Johnson's mother, Lela Bryant Johnson, a seamstress and domestic worker who supported the family during the Great Depression.

news. The Hurleys, the family that she and Dovey worked for, were pulling up stakes and moving—to Atlanta. The Hurleys wanted Lela and Dovey to come with them. Lela outlined a plan to Grandma Rachel: They would move to Atlanta, living in a safe neighborhood under the protection of the Hurleys, who were good, decent white people. They would work and save for two years, until they had enough money to pay for Dovey's first year at Spelman. When Dovey's place on campus was secured, Lela would return to Charlotte.

Rachel, unconvinced, remained quiet. She meditated and prayed and listened patiently, day after day, as her daughter pleaded her case. Finally Rachel gave her blessing. Dovey was her granddaughter, after all; she was made of strong stuff. With the matter settled, Dovey set her sights on the future. She thought she might become a doctor. Why shouldn't she use her mind to ease others' pain? She would study and grow and, in time, do her part to heal the world.

CHAPTER 2

UNDER THE SPELL OF SPELMAN

The Hurleys' new home was in Decatur, fifteen miles outside Atlanta. Lela and Dovey would ride the trolley into the city and stroll across Spelman's spacious lawns to remind themselves why they had left Charlotte. Amid the soaring columns and majestic magnolias of the campus, Dovey felt closer than ever to the world she'd been dreaming of. Little did she and Lela know that enrolling at Spelman would be only half the battle. The real victory would be staying there.

Even surrounded by the beauty of Spelman, Dovey never failed to notice the crumbling neighborhoods surrounding the campus. The college was an island in a sea of misery: Men in shabby clothes roamed the streets of Atlanta, looking for jobs that didn't exist; children slept in alleyways while their mothers searched for food amid piles of garbage. The Hurleys' home in Decatur provided welcome relief.

After toiling for two years for the Hurleys, Dovey and her mother finally saved up the seventy-five dollars for tuition. Reluctantly Lela packed up and returned to Charlotte, leaving her daughter to fend for herself and continue working for the Hurleys on her own. It was 1934, and Dovey was twenty years old.

Almost as soon as Lela left, Mrs. Hurley changed. Before, she had always been kind to Dovey. Now she began to resent her and question why she wanted to enroll in college. When Dovey showed Mrs. Hurley her letter of acceptance to Spelman, the woman looked as if she wanted to snatch it and tear it to pieces. Dovey tried to focus on taking care of the Hurleys' son, Bailey Jr. Just six years old, he hadn't yet learned to hate.

Dovey soon found herself racing out of the house to class as soon as she could in the morning. When she returned in the evening, she tended to her chores before

Dovey Johnson as a senior at Spelman College, 1938.

studying until she couldn't keep her eyes open any longer. Meanwhile, Mrs. Hurley and her friends became openly disdainful, calling Dovey "impudent" and suggesting that she didn't know her place. "Something inside me began to harden," Dovey recalled years later. "I understood that in all the years when she'd talked so proudly of how she would 'make something' of me, she had not imagined I would actually try to make something of *myself*."

Ever watchful of Mrs. Hurley, Dovey maintained an impassive expression, determined to give nothing away.

"Never in my life had I hidden my thoughts and feelings, but now, alone in a house where I was despised, I drew up a mask and I took care never to let it slip in Mrs. Hurley's presence," Dovey later said.

Off campus, Dovey delighted in attending Sunday dinners at the home of Maggie Wimbish. The mother of Dovey's eighth-grade teacher, Mrs. Wimbish was one of the most influential Black women in all of Atlanta. Her gatherings ensured three things: excellent food, elegant surroundings, and exciting company. She brought together teachers, lawyers, principals, professors, preachers, doctors—more accomplished, confident Black people than Dovey had ever seen.

One of Mrs. Wimbish's frequent guests, pastor and community leader Rev. James Madison Nabrit, inspired Dovey by telling her about his mother, Margaret Petty Nabrit. She had been one of Spelman's very first students, part of a group of eleven women who'd attended class in the basement of Friendship Baptist Church. Hearing such stories helped Dovey appreciate the rich tradition she had joined and made her even more determined to remain at Spelman until she had a diploma firmly in her grasp.

What's more, being with people like Mrs. Wimbish and Rev. Nabrit was a liberating experience. As wide as her grandparents' reach had been in Charlotte in Grandpa's early years at East Stonewall, Dovey had never been exposed to a world as sophisticated as the one in which the Wimbish family moved. The distinguished Black people who gathered at their home each Sunday were not only wealthy but also deeply committed to education. Within Maggie Wimbish's circle, Dovey felt comfortable enough to take off the mask she wore in the Hurleys' home and be herself: a young woman passionately in love with learning.

On campus, Dovey found another mentor, one as wise and kind and generous as Maggie Wimbish, with one significant difference: Mary Mae Neptune was white. "She was six feet tall, or close to it," Dovey remembered, "and every bit of sixty years old, with her white hair done up in a bun, but for all her old-fashionedness, Mae Neptune was without question a revolutionary, decades ahead of her time."

In middle age she had walked away from a long, successful career at traditionally white colleges and marched through Spelman's great iron gates. In her freshman English

Mary Mae Neptune, Spelman College
professor who mentored Dovey Johnson.

class, she challenged her students to dig deeply into literature, to analyze and dissect the great works until they reached a true understanding of them. From the very beginning, she singled out Dovey, recruiting her for the campus newspaper staff on the basis of her first composition. "Would you like to write for the paper, Miss Johnson?" she scrawled in red ink across the bottom of the essay. "You write well enough to!" For Dovey, Miss Neptune's support offered a powerful antidote to the hostile white world of the Hurley home. In one place, she was despised for daring to think for herself. In the other, she was encouraged—urged, even—to think with all her might.

Miss Neptune threw wide the doors to a world thousands of miles beyond Spelman's gates. This was the fall of 1934, five years before World War II broke out in Europe, but Adolf Hitler, the new chancellor of Germany, was quietly beginning his campaign to build his Thousand Year Reich by expanding Germany's borders. In the pages of the *New York*

Times, which Miss Neptune insisted her students read, Dovey tracked Hitler's campaign to absorb a tiny piece of land on the German-French border called the Saar Basin. She discovered that Hitler and his Nazi Party henchmen were taking over the region's newspapers and turning them into Nazi propaganda machines. She read about how they sent terror troops called the SS into the little country's capital on the eve of their so-called free election, in which the citizens were to vote whether to become part of Nazi Germany or of France. She shuddered when she read the headlines on the morning after the election, in which the people of the Saar Basin voted to become Nazis. The details were disturbing and complicated.

But there was a way to understand them, Miss Neptune told Dovey, and that was by writing about them until the truth became clear. As Dovey threw herself into research for the term paper on the Saar Basin that Miss Neptune assigned her, she came to see that what had caused the Saarlanders to cast their "free" votes to join Nazi Germany was the same kind of intimidation she'd known since she was a little girl. She began to look at racism in a new light—as something larger, more menacing than she'd ever imagined. Under Miss Neptune's guidance, she found herself reaching and digging deeply, stretching her mind.

Everywhere she turned on the campus, Dovey found professors who challenged and pushed her the way Miss Neptune did. The goal of the college was to turn young Black women into independent thinkers and committed leaders. The nation's oldest historically Black liberal arts college for women, Spelman had been founded in 1881 as Atlanta Baptist Female Seminary, before changing its name in 1884. As a double major in English and biology, immersed in and nurtured by brilliance on all sides, Dovey felt joyously baptized "into the life of the mind." She was, she later said, as eager as "a half-crazy rabbit turned loose in a briar patch, so wild with excitement at the things that were mine for the taking I barely knew what to grab first."

While composing an essay on American democracy for Miss Neptune, Dovey recalled, "I saw, as I scribbled furiously far into the night, that ever since I'd been old enough to eavesdrop on Grandma's church ladies whispering about lynchings and Klan burnings and Black men disappearing for who knew what reason, I'd been soaking up one long lesson in democracy gone wrong. I wrote as though someone had opened the floodgates, about the uneven hand of justice in the 'land of the free' and the grotesque thing called 'separate but equal,' putting into words thoughts I hadn't known were mine."

But there was a lighter, less intense, more joyful side to those early Spelman days, and Dovey found respite and happiness in the most improbable of all places: on the dreaded trolley cars of Atlanta. Riding home one day, she looked up from her book and noticed a handsome young man admiring her from across the aisle. His name was Bill Roundtree, he said, and he was a student at Morehouse College, Spelman's brother school. Dovey discovered that, unlike the majority of wealthy Morehouse men, Bill was a working student from a background almost as modest as her own, a person who knew what it meant to hold down a job to make ends meet. They formed a bond quickly and began timing their library sessions to coincide. She enjoyed being with Bill, took delight in his warmth and his sense of humor and his awe at her dreams of medical school. But the fact was that books were her favorite companions. When surrounded by them, every-thing else fell away. "Looking back on those heady times from a distance of years," she later remembered, "I see so clearly that my real love affair was with ideas."

Ideas were always on display at nearby Atlanta Univer-sity. In its lecture halls, some of the boldest African American thinkers of the time held forth on issues of great importance to their communities and to the nation at large. Dovey sat in a packed auditorium and heard the revered sociologist and historian W. E. B. Du Bois outline his vision of a future in which Black citizens lived free and equal lives. Explaining his theory of the Talented Tenth, he described an elite class of educated Black Americans leading the entire race to freedom and prosperity. He also talked about the "terrible twoness," a sense of division that some Black people experienced as they navigated white society. From him and other scholars,

Famed sociologist W. E. B.
Du Bois, whose speeches at Atlanta
University inspired Dovey
Johnson during her Spelman
College years and beyond.

she came to a broader understanding of her people's journey
through American history.

Dovey:

*I divined a portrait of my race that made me proud
beyond the telling. I came to see that the struggle for
dignity and respect and equal treatment wasn't only
about me. And it wasn't about today. There was
an "us" that spanned centuries and continents, that
was far bigger than one hundred years of slavery
and the degradation of Jim Crow.*

*No young Black person who listened to Du Bois
say that we were "equal to every living soul on*

the face of the earth" could remain unchanged.
To stand tall, tall in your blackness: That was the
call he sounded. His ideas held a healing power,
and so did my long discussions of them with Miss
Neptune.

Dovey admired the way Du Bois channeled his anger. Instead of letting it distract him or pull him down, he used it as a mighty tide that swept him forward.

But all of Dovey's forward motion, all her excitement and sense of progress, came to a violent, crashing halt one horrible May afternoon at the Hurley home. She arrived to find Mrs. Hurley yelling and screaming, her shrieks piercing the stillness. With little Bailey Jr. crouching fearfully in the corner, his mother waved her arms frantically and accused Dovey of stealing. Mrs. Hurley was so hysterical that Dovey couldn't make out the details. Before she could gain some sense of her situation, she was arrested and escorted out of the house. Behind her she could hear Mrs. Hurley wailing as if the world were coming to an end.

The only world in danger of ending was Dovey's. For all her careful behavior, for all her dutiful labor and diligent studying, she had still ended up where no Black American ever wanted to be. She was locked up tight in a southern jail, a no-man's-land where people like her were known to disappear without a trace. Struggling to think clearly despite her terror, she quickly concluded that none of her Black friends, regardless of their status, had any chance of helping her. She was permitted a single phone call. So she turned to the one white person she had learned to trust: Miss Neptune.

Hours passed before a white man arrived at the jail-house. He was an attorney, he said, sent by Mae Neptune and Spelman treasurer Phern Rockefeller. The lawyer, Slye Howard, secured Dovey's release the next morning. He instructed her to consider the matter settled and to think no more of it. She was free and her name was clear, but that solved only part of her problem. Banished from the Hurley home, she had no money and no place to live.

For the next two years and over two summers, Dovey ran more than she walked across Spelman's campus, working two, then three, jobs to stay afloat. She cleaned dormitories, did research for Miss Neptune, and worked as a lab assistant in the biology department, all of which enabled Dovey to cover room and board in a tiny house near campus. But it wasn't enough for much of anything else, including tuition. As the Depression deepened, even some of the wealthy girls began leaving school.

As her junior year wound to a close, the president of the college, Florence Read, called Dovey to her office. In such hard economic times, she explained, Spelman could not afford to carry any student. Miss Read recommended that Dovey take a teaching job and save enough to pay off her debt and re-enter the college. There was another option, but it was a painful one: Dovey would have to pay off her debt immediately or leave school at the end of the semester.

It was May 1937. As far as Dovey knew, she was all out of options. The teaching job she'd been encouraged to pursue would never pay enough to enable her return through Spelman's gates. Besides, it was time she helped her family, after all the sacrifices they'd made for her. She wandered in a daze, not really realizing where she was heading. When she finally looked up, she discovered she was standing in front of Miss Neptune's apartment building.

Unable to speak at first, Dovey stood weeping in her professor's apartment, finally managing to make her dilemma clear. The wise English professor swung immediately into action. She made some calls, knocked on a few doors, and within hours Dovey found herself in the office of Spelman treasurer Phern Rockefeller, where the treasurer had been joined by a gentleman introduced to Dovey as John Stanley. There was a feeling of unreality about the scene and the events that unfolded before her, a feeling that she was in the midst of a strange dream.

Dovey stared as Miss Rockefeller explained the arrangements that would make it possible for Dovey to continue her studies at Spelman. The first part of the arrangement was a scholarship from the university. The second was a loan from Miss Neptune. Dovey shook off her amazement long enough to sign the documents placed before her. "Even in a state of shock . . . I understood the magnitude of what they had done," Dovey said. "Three white people who were no kin to me had seen fit to find money, somewhere, money that even a wealthy institution like Spelman surely needed in those hard times."

It had all come to pass because of Miss Neptune, the boldest white person she had ever known. Despite the professor's modest circumstances and a failing economy, Miss Neptune had put her own money on the line, investing in a future that was far from certain. Her generosity had made a way out of no way, as Grandma Rachel would have put it.

Dovey:

> There is always someone, I am convinced, who would be the miracle maker in your life, if you but believe. Miss Neptune was that person for me.
>
> She had made the impossible happen. It was Miss Neptune who'd approached Miss Rockefeller, who had in turn gone to President Read. She had taken on the authorities at Spelman in my behalf, at a time when scholarship funds were almost nonexistent. An elderly teacher on a modest salary, she'd used her personal savings to pay the balance of my tuition, and with precious little chance of recovering her money, given how bleak my prospects were in 1937.

Indeed, four years would pass before I was able to pay a single dollar on that loan, and another four before I presented Miss Neptune with the final installment—in a neat stack of bills, carefully folded and tucked in my bosom. Yet I knew even from the first that I could never compensate her, for what she had given me had no price.

As I stood stammering in Miss Rockefeller's office, promising over and over again to "repay every dime and then some," Miss Neptune had shaken her head and spoken three words that amounted to a lifetime charge. Though I couldn't know how, or when, or through whom I would execute the directive she issued on that May morning, I embraced it almost as a creed.

"Pass it on, Dovibus!" she told me, looking straight at me over her spectacles and smiling as I handed the papers across the desk to Mr. Stanley. "Pass it on!"

CHAPTER 3

IN THE ARMY NOW

At each step in her journey, Dovey had been lifted up by strong, brilliant, and fearless women. First there had been her grandmother Rachel and her mother, Lela; then Edythe and Maggie Wimbish, followed by Miss Neptune. The next woman to extend a guiding hand was none other than Mary McLeod Bethune, who had inspired Dovey from the time she was a little girl, watching the great woman in awe as she sat in the family parlor with Grandma. It was Dr. Bethune's example, more than any other, that had made Dovey believe in what she could achieve with an education. And it was Dr. Bethune whom Dovey sought out as she struggled to find her way forward in the years after her Spelman graduation.

She'd taken a teaching job in a little South Carolina town

called Chester, and although she took joy in the eagerness of her eighth-grade students, she began to feel that she belonged somewhere else. The daily radio dispatches from Europe tracked the terrifying movements of Hitler as he invaded Poland in September 1939, beginning the war that had been coming since Dovey had written about the Nazis' earliest movements during her freshman year at Spelman. Every week, it seemed, the news grew worse: Denmark fell, then Norway. And in the spring of 1940, during Dovey's second year of teaching, Germany marched into Holland, Belgium, and Luxembourg. With the world charging forward, Dovey felt she could no longer remain tucked away in the tiny town of Chester.

"More than at any time in my life, a great restlessness took hold of me," she recalled of that time. "As if drawn by a magnet, I began turning my thoughts in the direction where thousands were streaming in the 1940s—northward, toward jobs in the big cities, where factories now turned out tanks and airplanes." Civil rights leaders had persuaded President Franklin Delano Roosevelt to ban race discrimination in the defense industry. This, Dovey believed, afforded her the kind of new beginning she was seeking. She resigned her post, bade farewell to her family, and boarded a train to the nation's capital.

She arrived in 1941, among thousands of African Americans heading in the same direction.

To defeat Hitler, the United States would need tanks, planes, and weapons—and workers to build them. The president's executive order also provided for a Fair Employment Practices Committee (FEPC) to make sure that companies and labor unions with government contracts opened their doors to Black applicants. For the first time, Washington became the home of an expansive job market for people like Dovey.

Perhaps even more important, the nation's capital was also the home of Dr. Bethune. By this time she had become president of the National Council of Negro Women (NCNW), an influential civil rights group, and also served as an adviser to President Roosevelt and director of the Division of Negro Affairs of the National Youth Administration (NYA). The convener of the president's so-called Black Cabinet, she was sometimes referred to as the "First Lady of the Struggle." Her private residence in northwest Washington doubled as the headquarters of the NCNW. She presided over the organization's business from an upstairs office, where she warmly greeted the young lady who'd shown up bearing greetings from her grandmother.

"You're Rachel Graham's granddaughter," she said, extending her hand. "Turn around, child, and let me look at you!" Dr. Bethune's melodious voice and precise speech were well known throughout Black America, and Dovey felt thrilled to be on the receiving end of her eloquence. The activist and stateswoman listened as well as she spoke, allowing Dovey to talk in detail about her thwarted plans for medical school and her desire to help her family. She asked Dr. Bethune about jobs in the defense industry, but to her surprise, the older woman discouraged her. "No," she said, shaking her head. "I have something else in mind. And in the meantime, I need you. There are things for you to do right here."

After arriving with no prospects and hat in hand, Dovey left with a job. As Dr. Bethune's personal assistant, she spent much of each day clipping articles about her boss and her work from Black newspapers such as the *Chicago Defender*, the *Pittsburgh Courier*, and the *New York Amsterdam News*.

Dovey:

> *Every clip was logged into her files, as were the statistics she charged me with ferreting out and placing at her fingertips for the moment when she might need them in her fight for better schools, better housing, better lives for children. I watched her turn those cold numbers into tools, working them into letters to this or that official, citing them in phone conferences, packing them away in her briefcase for meetings at her NYA headquarters across town, slipping them into discussions with the colleagues*

*who sought her out in the council office for support
and advice.*

From her front-row seat in a corner of the office, Dovey
became a wide-eyed witness to history, marveling at the procession of famous personalities moving in and out of the
NCNW brownstone. While she worked, people like Walter
White, an NAACP leader, and Lester Granger, head of the
Urban League, huddled with Bethune in the cramped space
to debate policies and review proposals. Dr. Bethune's tireless

First Lady Eleanor Roosevelt (center) with Mary McLeod
Bethune (left), National Youth Administration director of
Negro affairs, and NYA executive director Aubrey Williams.

dedication raised tens of thousands of dollars for civil rights causes and influenced discussions in the White House.

That famous residence at 1600 Pennsylvania Avenue was the home of the most notable of Dr. Bethune's many visitors. Eleanor Roosevelt, First Lady of the United States, talked frequently with her, by phone and in person. Mrs. Roosevelt's crusades against lynching and segregation, as well as her fund-raising for Bethune-Cookman College, had brought her praise and even reverence in some African American circles. Nevertheless, she conducted herself at the council office as if she were an ordinary citizen. During Dovey's eight months as Dr. Bethune's assistant, she never grew completely used to hearing the First Lady greet her by her first name.

And yet for all Dr. Bethune's closeness to Mrs. Roosevelt and the power she wielded as head of the Black Cabinet, she couldn't sit in the front of the bus, dine at a white lunch counter, or quench her thirst at a water fountain reserved for whites.

The humiliations Dr. Bethune had to endure infuriated Dovey. It made no sense that a nation—in its capital city, no less—would subject its citizens to such injustices, while claiming to be devoted to freedom and democracy. The more Dovey thought about it, the angrier she became. Often her thoughts turned to the great orators she had heard during her student days in Atlanta. Du Bois and other scholars had argued that Black minds, properly trained and conditioned, were the most effective weapon in the battle against injustice. Remembering their cool passion and steely resolve, she pledged that she would not lose her temper or her faith. After all, hadn't her mother and grandmother told her that she was destined to do great things?

Meanwhile, other forces were at work on the world stage. Japan bombed Pearl Harbor, a US naval base in Hawaii, on December 7, 1941. More than 2,400 Americans died in the surprise assault. Four days later, Germany and Italy, allied with Japan, declared war against the United States. American soldiers, Black as well as white, headed overseas by the tens of thousands. To fight a war on two oceans and four continents, the country needed every available man, regardless of race. But not even the crisis of war wiped out Jim Crow. Black men could fight, Congress decided, but they must do so in separate units.

This prejudice against African Americans in the military stretched back to the days of the American Revolution, when white officers had argued against providing guns to African Americans who wanted to fight alongside them in battle. These officers said that Black people were not to be trusted with firearms, that they were cowardly and slow-witted.

In truth, Black people had served America courageously for centuries. Peter Salem, Nero Hawley, and others had performed heroically during the American Revolution. During the Civil War, fought over slavery, the nearly all-Black Fifty-Fourth Massachusetts Volunteer Infantry was praised for its fearlessness. In

Soldiers of the famed World War I "Harlem Hellfighters," the 369th Infantry Regiment.

World War I, the African American 369th Infantry Regiment, known as the Harlem Hellfighters, spent more time in continuous combat than any other American unit.

None of that mattered to the military's white leaders, who held firm on segregated units as World War II got underway. But Dr. Bethune, backed up by labor activist A. Philip Randolph and other Black leaders, mounted a countercharge. Just weeks after Pearl Harbor, she blasted the army's segregation policy in a *Pittsburgh Courier* column in which she proclaimed, "This is America's War," she asserted, "and We, Too, are Americans."

Sitting in her corner of Dr. Bethune's office listening to her in close conference with Eleanor Roosevelt, Dovey realized with pride, and some shock, that Bethune's "We" included not only Black men, but women too—women of all races. The fight seemed unwinnable, given how resistant the country's leaders had been to allowing women in the military. Only pure desperation in the wake of Pearl Harbor had persuaded the army to create the Women's Army Auxiliary Corps (WAAC) in order to build a stateside workforce to free up men to fight overseas. But African American women? At that, the army balked.

That was when Dovey saw just how fearless and determined Dr. Bethune really was. Refusing to take a "No" from the military on the subject of African American women, Bethune took up her cause with Mrs. Roosevelt, in the privacy of her office. As Dovey listened to the two women wrestling with the details, she saw that the First Lady was truly frightened of what might happen if Black women arrived on bases along with whites. The Black press had begun reporting racial incidents on military bases even before Pearl Harbor.

Back and forth Dr. Bethune and Mrs. Roosevelt went, until at last Dr. Bethune confronted the reluctant First Lady with a question she couldn't answer: "What am I going to tell my girls?" Mrs. Roosevelt grew quiet. And then she said, "Don't tell them anything yet, Mary. Give me some time."

Dovey never knew just what the First Lady did behind the scenes to make a way for Black women in the first class of 440 officer candidates. But within a matter of days, it was agreed that 40 Black women would enter—10 percent of the total, as was the case with men—and although they would be segregated in their own company, the entire class would train together. This, Dovey realized, was what Dr. Bethune had meant when she'd told her, "I have something else in mind for you." How proud she felt, to be chosen for such a historic task. She was frightened, but greater than her fear was her sense of obligation to Dr. Bethune, and to America. This was a way to crack the wall of Jim Crow, to do her part in what the press called the Double V Campaign—a movement to win social justice abroad *and* at home.

On July 20, 1942, she arrived at Fort Des Moines and joined the thirty-eight other Black women ultimately accepted for training. They soon gathered in the protective presence of Dr. Bethune. Having been appointed civilian adviser to the WAAC, she was on hand to reassure the recruits and ease their entry into a new and difficult world. She chose her words carefully, as she always did, comforting her young charges while building their confidence for the five weeks ahead. Much was at stake. These women, handpicked by Bethune, were recent graduates of southern colleges, and they represented the entire Black community in the United States, fourteen million strong.

Captain Dovey Johnson with Mary McLeod Bethune at a
Women's Army Corps luncheon, circa 1943-44.

Yet Dr. Bethune remained calm. "Here at Fort Des Moines, we have democracy in action," she told them. "We are seeking equal participation. We are not going to be agitators." Dovey would return often to those words in the days to come.

Dr. Bethune had more to say when Dovey walked her to her car. "I know that you understand very clearly why you are here," she said. "You must see to it that the others do not forget. I'm counting on you to do that."

Like her mentor, Dovey had embraced the Four Freedoms

that President Roosevelt had invoked as the nation moved toward war. A secure, democratic world depended on certain fundamental principles, he said, including freedom of speech, freedom of worship, freedom from want, and freedom from fear. Dovey's experiences in training camp provided more evidence of a fact she'd known all along: For people like her, freedom of any kind was seldom a simple or automatic thing. The discrimination she'd known all her life had reared its head when she boarded the army truck that shuttled recruits to camp. The driver had taken one look at her, the only Black woman in her group, and shunted her to the back seats. When she arrived at the fort, she'd confronted the same demeaning treatment. "Negroes on one side!" a white officer had shouted. "White women on the other!"

On the base, Dovey and her fellow recruits were told that they were defending a free way of life. She embraced the idea of freedom but found it undermined everywhere. Training films were shown in a segregated theater, and the Black women's first meals were eaten under COLORED signs on the mess hall tables. Dovey spoke out against the signs, and they were quickly taken down. But the army made it clear that it fully intended to segregate the races.

Dovey:

We received express orders to sit separately. That was Jim Crow the army way, and it hit hard.

Nothing personal could be shared: not gas masks or first aid supplies, not dining table space by day or the barracks by night, not the service club or the officers' club. And lest some dread disease pass from Black to white, the commandant decreed that after the Black women used the swimming pool for the hour allotted to us on Friday afternoons, the water must be not only cleaned but "purified."

In contrast, the city of Des Moines was not governed by a Jim Crow policy. Socially, Black Iowans kept to themselves. They lived in Black neighborhoods, worshipped at Black churches, and subscribed to Black newspapers. But neither shops nor restaurants nor movie theaters were segregated. On the base, Dovey and her fellow trainees began to ease across the fort's color line. Blacks and whites talked to one another, and many became comfortable in one another's company.

Yet two months after receiving her commission, Dovey bore painful witness as those first tentative steps toward genuine friendship collided with official army policy. During a meal at the Savery Hotel in Des Moines after a special training session, a white male officer became enraged at the sight of Black and white women chatting and eating together. He stormed through the cafeteria, scattering chairs, plates, and utensils. Black women grabbed their food and scurried out of his way, but they weren't moving fast enough to satisfy him. "You darkies move those trays," he ordered, "and sit where you belong!"

That night, Dovey and several of the other women met in a barracks to air their concerns. They had marched and drilled and saluted. They had responded to commands with attentive postures, sharp creases, and crisp salutes. They had stretched their tolerance and willingness to

Captain Dovey Johnson addressing potential WAC recruits, Akron, Ohio, 1944.

cooperate beyond normal expectations. But that final insult had pushed them to the breaking point.

Dovey recalled Dr. Bethune's assertion that their small group of officers represented all of Black America. With that in mind, she proposed sending a telegram to the woman whose efforts had brought them to Fort Des Moines in the first place. Her note to Dr. Bethune described the indignities they had endured since they'd arrived and specifically pointed out the "unnecessary prejudice" they had suffered in the dining hall at the Savery Hotel.

Ten women signed the telegram, but Dovey and an officer named Irma Cayton were identified as the ringleaders and summoned for discipline. Dovey suspected immediately that one of the other Black officers had betrayed them, noting years later, "The army, I would learn over time, cultivated such spies, using information thus obtained to isolate, intimidate, and even court-martial Blacks who challenged Jim Crow."

Summoning the two women to his office, the commandant denounced them as "agitators," the very thing that Dr. Bethune had said they were not. "You went outside military channels," he told them. "That amounts to treason."

Dovey and Irma remained cool, refusing to submit their resignations as the commandant demanded. To give in to his demands would be a betrayal of Dr. Bethune's efforts, to say nothing of the fourteen million African Americans whose hopes rested on their shoulders. "We might be agitators," Dovey told him, "but we are not traitors." She and Irma refused to resign. From then on, they were considered a threat to discipline and good order. Soon after, Dovey received orders sending her on a recruiting mission far from the base. She was assigned to find Black women recruits in Georgia, Florida, the Carolinas, and Texas. The army viewed Dovey's new task as punishment, but she saw it as the kind of challenge she'd been preparing for all her life.

She approached prominent pastors and appealed to them to reach out to ministers in every neighboring city

Dovey Johnson (right) and her WAC partner Ruth Lucas
organizing a 1944 campaign.

and town where they had friendly colleagues. She spread word of the WAAC before crowds at Black YMCAs, Black business associations, and NAACP meetings. Everywhere she went, she boldly told the truth about the pervasiveness of segregation in the army. She also talked about the virtues of military life, including the opportunities to advance and train for careers. Little did she know that the hopeful future she described would soon clash with the demeaning reality of her country's racist present.

That reality hit her full in the face late one night in a Miami bus station, when she was traveling on assignment alone. Recruiters often worked in pairs, but traveling together wasn't always possible. "I'd grown accustomed to watching my back on the recruiting trail," Dovey recalled, "where the army left us unescorted and unprotected, instructing us simply to 'be careful.'"

She entered the busy depot among a stream of soldiers and sailors. Like her, most were clad in their uniforms. Perhaps it was her feeling of solidarity with her fellow military personnel that led her to briefly forget the rules of Jim Crow and choose a bus seat reserved for whites. Perhaps she was thinking so much about her next recruiting trip that she was only dimly aware of the shouts punctuating the air around her. For whatever reason, it took her a while to realize the shouting was aimed at her. She looked up to see the driver yelling in her face. He ordered her to move and give her seat to another soldier, a grim white man standing by expectantly. At first, Dovey refused. "I am traveling on army business," she said, reaching into her duffel bag for her army papers and itinerary, "and I have orders to depart Miami by bus."

The Black passengers in the rear said nothing. They wanted to avoid trouble, and Dovey seemed to be looking for it. Her uniform alone, they knew, was enough to provoke angry whites to assault her—or worse. Black newspapers printed reports of Blacks in uniform being intimidated, shot, and sometimes lynched. The country had not wanted African Americans in the military, under any circumstances. To be a

Black soldier in the Deep South, especially one recruiting other soldiers, was to risk bodily harm.

Dovey's dignified manner enraged the driver even more. He forced her to get off and walk past a line of white army and navy personnel, who made no effort to help her or speak out on her behalf. They boarded the bus, which zoomed off in a blast of exhaust, leaving Dovey behind. She was forced to remain in the station for several hours until another bus came. During that time, she couldn't help recalling the streetcar incident from her childhood, when the driver had called her a pickaninny because she'd sat in the wrong seat. She waited and fumed, wrestling with a hatred deeper than any she'd ever felt—hatred of Jim Crow, hatred of the army, and hatred of fellow citizens who stood in silence or looked the other way while a racist driver denied her basic human rights.

She was still more than a little angry in August 1943, when she was preparing to reenlist as an officer in the Women's Army Corps (WAC), renamed when President Roosevelt signed a bill to remove the word *auxiliary* from the organization's name the preceding month. A month before she was to take the oath, the new commandant of Fort Des Moines announced his intention to completely segregate training of female recruits. Colonel Frank McCoskrie's plan called for Black officers to train other Blacks. They would in turn train the Black officers who came after them, ensuring that Black soldiers would be isolated for years to come.

Dovey's anger threatened to boil over into absolute fury. For nearly a year, she and her colleagues had been waiting for reenlistment in the WAC, whose members would be given full military status, with regular army ranks, and the associated pay and benefits. Like the rest of her comrades, Dovey saw the new WAC as a marvelous step forward. And yet she felt she had no choice, ethically, but to denounce the colonel's plan as an insult. It was unacceptable, she declared, and they had no choice but to oppose it. The women who agreed with Dovey appointed her their spokesperson in the meeting the commandant called to discuss his plan.

As the day approached, she determined that if the colonel proceeded with his plan, she would resign. She doubted that anyone else would decide to quit, but that didn't matter. Her grandmother had taught her the importance of standing up for what's right—even if it meant standing alone.

Dovey confronted the colonel at a crowded forum in the fort's auditorium. Rising from her seat, she unpinned her captain's bars, signaling to the colonel that she was willing to accept court-martial and the dishonorable discharge that would inevitably follow as a consequence of her defiance.

"Sir, you are setting us back a hundred years," she charged. "Can you actually believe that the advantages of this proposal can outweigh the damage it will cause?" She went on to argue that a Jim Crow regiment would fly in the face of the racism, tyranny, and oppression that Americans were fighting against overseas. What were our troops fighting for if not freedom, justice, and equality?

Silence filled the auditorium when she finished, and the barracks were equally quiet while Dovey and her fellow officers awaited the colonel's response. Four days later, silence, uncertainty, and fear of retaliation gave way to jubilation when Colonel McCoskrie reversed his position: The Jim Crow regiment wouldn't happen after all. Dovey had won.

The lessons she'd learned at the feet of her grandmother, in Mae Neptune's classroom, and in Dr. Bethune's Washington brownstone had all come together in one fateful moment. Dovey was still angry when she went back on the road to resume recruiting, but she was also deeply changed. She had seen the way in which a single voice—her voice—could make a difference.

Dovey:

> *Change steals over you when you're looking to the right, or the left, or far out ahead at the heavens somewhere, and then, at some point, you look inward and find yourself different. So it was with my time in the army. I entered the military a girl doing the bidding of others, living out the dream of a great leader, and marching to her orders. I left it a woman grown.*

Dovey Johnson shortly after her commissioning as an officer in the first class
of the newly formed Women's Army Corps.

When Dovey started out as a recruiter in 1942, fewer than 200 Black women had enlisted in the army. Before the war ended, 6,500 Black women had served in the WAC, far more than the army had anticipated. Some of them had even received assignments overseas. Among those were members of the 6888th Central Postal Directory Battalion, 855 women who'd served as postal workers, cooks, mechanics, and nursing assistants. The ranks of Black female applicants had swelled largely as a result of the efforts of Dovey and her fellow African American recruiters. They'd sought potential soldiers in places where other recruiters might not have known to look. They'd placed notices in local Black newspapers, promoted the war effort on radio, and visited every church, college, and Black organization willing to host them. Canvassing the country required its own kind of bravery, and these pioneering women had demonstrated their courage by doing their utmost to make the world safe for democracy. As one of the first women of any race to be commissioned an army officer, Dovey had made history. It wouldn't be the last time.

CHAPTER 4

HUNGRY MIND

Revelers lined both sides of Broadway, laughing, crying, and hugging. From the windows of tall buildings, New Yorkers tossed stream after stream of confetti. The curls of paper twisted and wound through the air in colorful clouds, settling on shoulders and hair before finally gathering on the ground like piles of glitter. Alongside thousands of Americans hollering "Hallelujah!" and "Hip hip hooray!" Dovey clapped her hands, yelling joyfully at the top of her lungs.

The United States declared victory over Japan on August 15, 1945, ending World War II. Celebrations like the one Dovey attended in New York were held for weeks throughout the country. With her sister Bea and her brother-in-law Gene, she saluted the return of the great general Jonathan

Wainwright, who had been taken prisoner in the Philippines. Her grandmother had always told her that ladies never shouted, but Dovey felt comfortable casting that advice aside. The war was over, and the United States had come out on top. Had there ever been a better time to shout? It made her heart glad to raise her voice to the heavens. She had spoken up for justice in the army, had told the truth while looking into the eyes of powerful people, captains and commandants who could have destroyed her future with the stroke of a pen. *Perhaps*, she thought, *I was born to make noise*.

The other African Americans dancing and laughing along Broadway felt the same triumphant spirit. They had reason to

A World War II victory parade similar to the one Dovey Johnson attended in New York after the US victory over Japan.

hope that their people's contribution to the war effort would lead to genuine progress. Real change seemed long overdue after a centuries-long struggle for freedom. The great poet and songwriter James Weldon Johnson had described the winding, dangerous path of African Americans through history in the poem "Lift Every Voice and Sing," whose words Dovey had loved since she was a little girl. "Stony the road we trod," Johnson had written in 1900. After his brother J. Rosamond Johnson set the poem to music in 1905, it was embraced by the NAACP and Black people across the country and became known as the Negro National Anthem. The song urges listeners to continue over that stony road, to "march on until victory is won." Victory overseas had been achieved—half of the Double V Campaign—but what about victory over Jim Crow? That battle was still underway, and Dovey was determined to remain in the fight.

She had yet to figure out exactly how she would do that. She was still hoping to enroll in medical school. She planned to pay her fees by taking advantage of the GI Bill of Rights. It provided funds for education to all interested veterans, including Black ones. Even with her money problems mostly solved, her options would be limited. Nashville's Meharry Medical College and Howard University's medical school in Washington, DC, were the only institutions of their kind that could be trusted to open their doors to qualified African American students.

As she weighed her options, Dovey's mind turned to a gathering she had attended during the war at the home of one of her WAC recruits. On that occasion, Dovey's impassioned discussion of the Double V Campaign had attracted the attention of A. Philip Randolph, one of several distinguished activists in attendance. He'd made his way to the front of the circle and listened intently while Dovey spoke. When she'd finished talking, he offered her his card. "I'm A. Philip Randolph," he'd said. "I'd like it very much if you looked me up after the war."

A few days after the parade, Dovey visited his office in New York. Randolph explained that the Fair Employment Practices Committee was on shaky ground. Congress had cut its budget by half, and its sixteen offices around the country had been reduced to three. He was on a mission to save his remaining bureaus and persuade Congress to pass a law making the FEPC a permanent agency. The

Revered labor activist A. Philip Randolph, head of the Fair Employment Practices Committee (FEPC), for which Dovey Johnson worked in 1945–46.

FEPC had been established by President Roosevelt to secure defense-industry jobs for African Americans. It owed its existence to Randolph, who had threatened to organize a hundred thousand Black citizens and lead them in a march on the nation's capital. Under his careful supervision, the FEPC had helped triple the number of Black citizens working in industry and government. With the war over, support for the committee was dwindling fast.

The FEPC was just one of Randolph's projects. He had long been lobbying for a fully integrated military, and he'd fought for wage equality as founder of the Brotherhood of Sleeping Car Porters, the nation's first Black labor union. These accomplishments had earned him widespread admiration among his fellow African Americans. Approaching Congress wouldn't be enough, he told Dovey. FEPC representatives needed to sweep across the nation, speaking on behalf of the committee to local councils and grassroots organizations. They needed to persuade people to help get state laws passed. Randolph envisioned a coalition of people of all races, striving together to help Black workers. If they failed, millions could lose their jobs. In his view, few rights were more sacred than the right to work.

Randolph, always attired in a suit and tie and inclined to speak in deep, formal tones, had often persuaded powerful people to see things his way. Dovey was just as moved. Within an hour of visiting him, she'd agreed to work for the FEPC. Using the skills she'd developed in the army, she would carry out Randolph's mission in West Coast cities such as San Francisco, Los Angeles, and Portland. The dangers she would face would differ from those in the South, where most lynchings and other acts of racist terror were committed, but press reports indicated a high risk of hostility and even bodily harm in her assigned region.

Her intention was to work for the FEPC for six months and then enroll in medical school. That was the plan she shared with her mother and grandmother during a brief visit home to Charlotte. It was a temporary assignment, she told them, and after training as a physician, she'd be back for good. It was a golden autumn day, and as she listened to the voices of the women who had raised her, she felt torn between the comfort of home and the causes to which she had become devoted. She remembered the same conflicting emotions in college while listening to W. E. B. Du Bois talk about the con-flicts educated African Americans would experience when they left their familiar communities to face the challenges of the world at large. Sitting in the audience, Dovey had known instinctively what Du Bois meant. She was not only a Black woman preparing for life in a white world but also a woman training for a professional career, far from her working-class roots. Nestled in a comfortable swing on her family's front porch, she struggled to overcome those nagging doubts. Who was she working for if not her family?

Seven years had passed since she'd graduated from Spelman. It had been nearly as long—four years—since she'd spoken with Bill Roundtree. They were no longer sweethearts, but they had managed to stay in touch. He had written to her throughout the war, sending postcards and notes even after he was assigned to a post in Europe. Back home after the war ended, he called the Graham family homestead more than once to ask about Dovey. Each time, her mother or grandmother passed along word of Bill's calls. Dovey felt a flutter that surprised her. Memories of their days together in college washed over her, and she made plans to reconnect with him before heading to the West Coast. But first she had someone else to see and a debt to settle.

Professor Mary Mae Neptune had retired to Decatur, the same town where Dovey had been exiled from the Hurley household and forced to fend for herself. Now Miss Neptune was in a similar position, on her own with barely enough retirement funds to get by. Her apartment consisted of a single room filled with run-down furniture, raggedy curtains, tattered rugs, and books. Volumes of Austen, Dickens, and Shakespeare crowded bookshelves from floor to ceiling.

As she had done with Bill, Dovey had remained in contact with her former mentor. Over the past seven years, she'd sent her payments on the loan. She tucked as much as she could into each envelope, sometimes just a dollar or two. After she entered the army, the envelopes she sent were considerably heavier. Miss Neptune never failed to write back. She supplemented her long letters with clippings from the *New York Times* and observations about current events. She commented on the war and expressed concern for Dovey's safety, but she never mentioned the loan.

Over tea, the old professor questioned her former student with all the attentiveness of a lawyer cross-examining a witness. Aware of the latest developments in the civil rights struggle, she was excited about Dovey's upcoming work with A. Philip Randolph. Finally, after several hours of warmhearted conversation, Dovey stood up to leave. Before heading for the door, she produced an envelope and placed it on the table. It contained all that she still owed on the loan.

Miss Neptune stared at Dovey with her customary directness. "What on earth is this, Dovey Johnson?" she finally asked.

"A sacred trust," Dovey replied. "All that I owe you and a little bit more." She watched as Miss Neptune pulled a sheaf of papers from a drawer. On top, *Loan, Mary Mae Neptune to Dovey Mae Johnson* was written in her careful hand. Dovey saw the neat rows of columns, each recording a payment she'd sent. Miss Neptune wrote *Paid in Full* across the columns and handed Dovey the papers. Dovey recalled the day she'd been turned away from school, her tearful stumble to Miss Neptune's apartment. Taking the papers in hand, she also grasped a fundamental truth about her relationship with her generous teacher. She may have repaid the loan, but she'd still be forever in her debt.

When Dovey spoke with Bill, she felt the years melt away until it seemed as if she were back at Spelman, keeping company with the handsomest man at Morehouse. The war had changed her in so many ways, pushing her toward the larger world but also deepening her longing to settle down, raise a family, return to "normal"—whatever that was. Quickly, they became a couple again, although Dovey was heading for work in San Diego, far from Bill's Atlanta home. They talked every day after she arrived there and made plans to meet in Chicago at Christmas.

In the meantime, Dovey plunged into work, racing from one FEPC council meeting to another throughout Southern California. When she had been an army recruiter, she spoke solely to other African Americans. In California, her audiences consisted of Blacks, whites, Latinos, Chinese, and Japanese. She learned that they often didn't trust one another, making A. Philip Randolph's dream of a multiracial campaign more difficult than either she or Randolph had imagined.

In many of the towns she visited, racial tensions ran high. The same was true of big cities, such as Los Angeles. Two years before she arrived, the so-called zoot suit riots had torn the city apart. White soldiers and sailors had gone on a

Armed sailors and marines during the June 1943 Los Angeles "zoot suit riots,"
in which American servicemen violently clashed with young Latino men.

rampage, targeting and assaulting young Mexican Americans
who favored zoot suits—outfits that featured long, loose jack-
ets with padded shoulders. They went on to attack African
Americans as well. Making matters worse, the Ku Klux Klan
was flourishing there, forcing people of color out of respect-
able communities and into dirty, unsafe neighborhoods.

While the racism Dovey encountered on the West Coast
often discouraged her, she also found reason for cheer. She
began to socialize with community activists, elected officials,
lawyers, law students, and other serious thinkers. Talking with

them about art, culture, and politics, she felt at home. Associating with this group led to her first close Southern California friendship, an alliance that would change her life and shift the direction of her future. In the fall of 1945, she met Pauli Murray, a gifted African American scholar at Berkeley Law. Murray would one day gain prominence as an advocate for full equality for women. She would go on to cofound the National Organization for Women and become one of the first women ordained to the priesthood in the Episcopal Church. Dovey had read the newspaper accounts of Murray's unsuccessful attempt to enroll in the University of North Carolina's grad-

Lawyer, minister, feminist, and civil rights activist Pauli Murray.

uate school several years earlier. Murray soon convinced Dovey that real justice for Black people could best be achieved through the law.

In their long conversations, Murray probed the history of Reconstruction, the period after the Civil War, when Congress had passed three important constitutional amendments. The Thirteenth, Fourteenth, and

Fifteenth Amendments had paved the way toward equality for
Black people by abolishing slavery, granting citizenship and
equal protection to everyone born in the United States, and
guaranteeing citizens the right to vote. Almost immediately,
however, state governments moved to weaken the amendments by passing Jim Crow laws. And in 1896, in a notorious case known as *Plessy v. Ferguson*, Murray explained,
the Supreme Court had made "separate but equal" the law
of the land. But she told Dovey that a fundamental change
was taking place in the courts. They were slowly returning
to the real meaning of the Reconstruction amendments. That
shift, Murray predicted, would finally lead to the death of Jim
Crow. Dovey listened and tried to imagine a world in which
Black people could live where they wanted, eat where they
wanted, worship where they wanted. She saw herself trying
on clothes in stores just as white people did. She saw a little
Black girl riding in a trolley car without being called insulting
names. She saw a Black woman soldier, newly commissioned
and smartly dressed in her crisp uniform, sitting proudly in
the front of a bus. When interpreted fairly, could laws make
all that happen? Perhaps they could.

Murray regarded the case of *Gaines v. Canada* as an
important step in the battle to end segregation. A young man
named Lloyd Gaines had applied for admission to the University of Missouri School of Law. The school rejected his
application because he was Black, offering to send him to

a comparable institution in another state. Gaines sued the school. Lawyers Charles Hamilton Houston and his protégé Thurgood Marshall had taken Gaines's case, and in three years it had gone all the way to the US Supreme Court. In 1938, the court had ruled in favor of Gaines, affecting not just Missouri but all sixteen states that prohibited Black students from enrolling. Houston and Marshall's victory meant that states had to provide Blacks with an equal legal education or allow them entry into whites-only law schools. The lawyers' campaign for enforcement of the ruling ended with the mysterious disappearance of Gaines, but the victory laid an important foundation. Using Gaines as a basis, the two lawyers took their fight to public schools in the South by building cases against individual school districts. Little by little, Houston's campaign against Jim Crow was gathering steam. "He's assembling an army at Howard University Law School," Murray said. "And you should be a part of it." Persuaded by the strength of her friend's arguments, Dovey began to turn away from thoughts of a medical career. The law was pulling her in like a piece of iron drawn to a magnet.

Meanwhile, she agreed to marry Bill in December 1946. The wedding would take place in Chicago, and as she rode the train there, she considered how much she had changed since first meeting him. Instead of a shy, unsure twenty-year-old, she was a thirty-two-year-old army veteran who had risked her career to speak out against injustice. She wondered how much Bill had changed in their seven years apart. Did they see the world in the same way? Did they share the same goals?

Dovey also wondered how her desire to have a family would mesh with her ambitious career plans. Her friend Pauli assured her that she could indeed have both. In the end, she chose to cast her doubts aside.

Soon after arriving in Chicago, Dovey Mae Johnson became Dovey Johnson Roundtree. With Dovey's WAC comrade Ruth Lucas and her fiancé as witnesses, Dovey and Bill exchanged vows as dusk fell on Christmas Eve. After the holidays, Bill accompanied Dovey to Portland, her last FEPC posting. She would be calling for Oregon legislators to pass a fair employment law to support a federal measure that would soon be proposed in Washington. At first, Bill accompanied her as she made her rounds. He sat up front proudly at local meetings, applauding whenever Dovey spoke out against racist laws and limited working opportunities.

In time, Bill's interest subsided, though, while Dovey's passion continued to increase. Obsessed with the civil rights revolution taking shape, she continued to advocate and organize for the cause. In contrast, Bill stayed home. Dovey tried to focus on the happy moments, but silence soon replaced joy in their tiny apartment. When Dovey finished her assignment and the couple moved to Washington, Bill revealed his intention to reenlist in the army. Law school, he told her, had been her dream, not his. It became clear that they were moving along different paths. The army had changed her profoundly, challenging her and setting her on a path she had not imagined during the years when she and Bill had courted as students. It was now painfully clear that they were two entirely different sorts of people. Dovey realized she had rushed into marriage, thinking that their happiness together would overcome any difficulties. As she contemplated her future, she concluded that she had been wrong to move so fast. Their union had been a terrible mistake.

It took Dovey a year to recover from the sorrow stemming from the breakup of her marriage. In the midst of her sadness, however, she realized how much she had changed. Gone was the hopeful, inexperienced young woman who had stepped uncertainly onto Spelman's campus. She had trod a "stony road" through war and marriage—and managed to stay on her feet. Pauli Murray's encouragement bolstered her confidence as she filled out the application to Howard Law School. Still, her friend's words only affirmed a truth she already felt deep in her bones, a truth she knew as well as she knew her name: She was Rachel Graham's granddaughter, and she was as good as anybody.

Dovey:

In choosing the law as a vocation . . . I was stepping into a lonely and dangerous arena, one in which a woman, particularly a Black woman, would stand out as something close to a freak . . . But I could not turn away from the law, once it took hold of me, any more than I could deny my own name, or my very being. I was thirty-three years old when I walked into the musty basement that housed the Howard University School of Law in September of 1947, and I was as hungry, and as certain of my course as I have ever been . . . I'd been derailed first by lack of money and then by the war. This time around, I vowed, nothing would stop me.

CHAPTER 5

JIM CROW MUST GO

By the time Dovey entered law school, she had endured enough indignities to fully appreciate the damage Jim Crow was inflicting on African Americans. But there was yet another layer of prejudice she'd felt closing in upon her, one that threw up walls for women. "Jane Crow," Pauli Murray had called it, the bias against women that slammed doors in their faces and imposed limits on their advancement. Dovey had seen it after her Spelman graduation, when she faced the harsh reality of medical school admission as a woman. And she'd confronted it in the military, in the scorn with which male officers dealt with all military women, Black and white alike. But somehow, the reality of Jane Crow took her by surprise when she found it waiting for her at Howard University School of Law.

Howard University students crossing the campus, where the law school was housed at the time Dovey enrolled.

She stepped up to the counter in the fall of 1947 to present her paperwork, including her certificate of honorable discharge from the army, expecting the process of GI Bill benefit qualification to be simple and quick. Instead, the clerk studied the documents as if she were unable to read them. Puzzled, she asked Dovey, "Are you registering for your husband or your brother?"

"No. I am the veteran named on the documents," Dovey replied. "The honorable discharge belongs to *me*. I am claiming GI benefits on my *own* behalf."

This time the clerk looked at Dovey as if she were speaking a foreign language and repeated her question: "Are you registering for your husband or your brother?"

The other clerks gathered around their colleague, staring at Dovey and her documents. Registration slowed to a halt. Dovey sighed, aware of the men glaring impatiently behind her. She began to fear that her registration would be delayed beyond the beginning of the semester, forcing her to catch up in all her classes. Finally she leaned across the counter and pointed to the blanks on her GI benefit form. "Do it just like you do it for the male veterans," she instructed.

Dovey was through the gates at last. She had yet to open a textbook, but she needed no legal training to know that Black people were increasingly exhausted—and angered—by having to endure second-class citizenship. They might not have been harassed during basic training or stranded at a Miami bus depot, as Dovey had, but they had undoubtedly suffered their own humiliating encounters. Dovey understood their rage as easily as she recalled her own. Of that night in Miami, she remembered, "I wrestled with hatred deeper than I'd ever known, hatred of Jim Crow, hatred of the army that had cast me adrift in hostile territory, and most of all, hatred of these people who had treated me as an interloper in my own country."

Charles Hamilton Houston also understood this rage. The

dean of Howard's law school declared war on Jim Crow in 1947. "There is no such thing as separate but equal," he proclaimed. He knew that activists and ordinary citizens alike had been fighting against it for years, through coordinated campaigns led by visionaries such as Du Bois, Randolph, and Bethune, as well as by individual acts of protest carried out at great risk. In his view, resistance was on the rise, weakening Jim Crow's defenses. It was time for African Americans to gather their forces and strike a fatal blow. Houston agreed with Pauli Murray: Law would be the weapon. The courts would be the battleground.

Houston had trained at Harvard Law School, one of the few African Americans to have done so. He assembled his team of litigators and scholars from the small group of Black attorneys who had also studied there, along with graduates of Howard and Northwestern. They'd prep for their epic Supreme Court contests by convening in Howard's library to pore over documents and exchange ideas. Afterward, they would rehearse oral arguments in the school's moot courtroom. Classes were held in the basement, where Dovey entered as one of five women in the first-year class.

She was dismayed but not surprised to learn that some men were unhappy to have her as a classmate. They behaved as if female students had unfairly taken places more properly reserved for men. When she walked up to a group of men, they would abruptly end their conversation, leaving an awkward silence. In class, men sometimes scoffed at comments that women offered, or they talked right over them. Some days Dovey felt as out of place as she had been when surrounded by white officers in the Fort Des Moines mess hall. Making friends in her new neighborhood of Garfield Heights, in the area of southeast Washington known as Anacostia, helped her overcome those challenges. So did her membership in Allen Chapel AME Church. The congregation had been named for Richard Allen, a former slave who'd founded the African Methodist Episcopal denomination in 1816. The warmth and hospitality of the parishioners reminded Dovey of the people she'd known and loved at her grandfather Clyde's church back in Charlotte. Their kindness encouraged her on difficult days and motivated her to keep up with her studies.

On campus, she benefited from the generous wisdom of Ollie Mae Cooper, executive secretary to the dean. Brilliant and industrious, she was one half of the first law firm founded by Black women in the entire country. Despite having two demanding jobs, she met regularly with the female students, checking on their progress, consoling them when they were down, and nudging them when they needed it. "You can do wonders to improve the practice of law," she told them. "It's in need of a woman's touch."

Inside the classroom, Professor James Madison Nabrit Jr. inspired Dovey in a way no other professor besides Mae Neptune ever had. The son of Rev. Nabrit, the prominent pastor she had met while at Spelman, he was a first-rate legal mind and a principal strategist in the NAACP's crusade for full equality. Nabrit had given up a private practice in Texas to consult with the nation's oldest civil rights organization while molding aspiring lawyers like Dovey. Almost ten years before, he had created the first civil rights course offered at any American law school.

Dovey had to juggle two part-time jobs while meeting the rigorous demands of teachers like Nabrit. To help her get through, she joined a study group led by a third-year student named Julius Winfield Robertson. Brilliant and confident, he was respected and admired by his peers. His esteem for Dovey influenced others to welcome her into their orbit. The five other members of their group soon became Dovey's second family. They met on weekends at her apartment in Garfield Heights. Sprawled among piles of textbooks spread all over the tiny space, they dissected cases and debated judicial decisions. Dovey stepped carefully around the mess, moving to the kitchen and back with a thick law volume in her hand. She spouted opinions while stirring up a pot of dinner for her hungry classmates. Mastering the law became the driving force of her life.

Her classes included Professor Nabrit's civil rights course, one of the law school's toughest offerings. His syllabus contained two thousand cases, which the students were expected to master. A giant in his field, Nabrit provided his students with an up close view of America's most pivotal conflict since World War II. That battle had taken place on foreign soil; this time the fighting would take place in the streets and courts of the United States. Because of Dovey's training at Howard, she would be more than a witness. She would be a participant, and she needed to be fully armed for the combat to come.

Famed civil rights lawyer and professor James Madison Nabrit Jr., who inspired Dovey
Roundtree as a professor during her years at Howard University School of Law.

She leaned forward in her seat in Nabrit's class, listening with rapt attention as he intoned the opening lines of the Fourteenth Amendment, which forbade the states from interfering with an individual's rights under US law:

"All persons born or naturalized in the United States, and subject to the jurisdiction thereof, are citizens of the United States and of the state wherein they reside. No state shall make or enforce any law which shall abridge the privileges or immunities of citizens of the United States; nor shall any state deprive any person of life, liberty, or property, without due process of law; nor deny to any person within its jurisdiction the equal protection of the laws."

Dovey recalled her sessions with Pauli Murray as she listened to Nabrit explain that when Reconstruction ended in 1877, the sixteen southern states had moved swiftly to limit the rights of their emancipated Black residents. To do so, they had to ignore not only the Fourteenth Amendment but also the Thirteenth, which abolished slavery and any form of enforced labor, and the Fifteenth, which guaranteed all citizens the right to vote regardless of their race.

The southern states fought these amendments with all their might, enacting laws of their own that separated the former slaves from white people and deprived them of their freedom. The Fourteenth Amendment guaranteed all citizens "equal protection," but the southern states took the position that separate neighborhoods, facilities, and schools for

Black people were equal to those that whites enjoyed. This policy became known as "separate but equal," even though the facilities provided to Blacks were in fact far inferior to those for whites.

For many African Americans, as Dovey well knew, one of the most inconvenient and humiliating separations was in the area of travel. All buses, trains, trolleys, and streetcars in the South were segregated, into Jim Crow cars on trains, or into separate sections on buses and trolleys. By the end of the 1800s, the South had such a rigid segregation system in place that Black leaders began to fear that if they did not push back, African Americans would never get out from under the iron hand of Jim Crow. They chose the area of train travel to launch their fight and formed committees in various states and cities across the South to mount attacks.

The most famous of these fights began in New Orleans, Louisiana, when the Citizens Committee enlisted a Black shoemaker named Homer Plessy to test the city's two-year-old Separate Car Act in the hope that they could win a court ruling against train segregation.

First-class ticket in hand, Homer Plessy boarded the East Louisiana Railway in New Orleans on June 7, 1892, bound for Covington, about forty miles away. Of mixed-race ancestry, Plessy was pale enough to enter the whites-only railcar without difficulty. When he told the conductor that he was part Black, he was yanked from the train and thrown in jail. After he was convicted, he filed a petition against the judge, John H. Ferguson. He argued that the law violated the equal protection clause of the Fourteenth Amendment. When the Louisiana court ruled against him, Homer Plessy took his case to the Supreme Court. He and the Citizens Committee hoped that the highest court in the United States would see the dishonesty of "separate but equal" and rule in their favor.

But their efforts backfired. On May 18, 1896, the Supreme Court ruled against him, setting in stone the practice of legally sanctioned segregation. In *Plessy v. Ferguson*, the court declared that separate accommodations for Black people were not inferior. If Blacks saw separate facilities as inferior, the court said, "it is not by reason of anything found in the [Separate Car] act but solely because the colored race chooses to put that construction upon it." In other words, the justices said that the perception of inferiority was completely in the minds of Black people and had nothing to do with the fact of segregation and substandard facilities. The court's decision in *Plessy v. Ferguson* affirmed African Americans' second-class status. For the next several decades, their right to travel, eat, use the bathroom, sleep, buy homes, and go to school would be severely limited.

Only one justice, John Harlan, supported Plessy's argument. In his basement classroom, Professor Nabrit held up

Harlan's dissent as a vision of the future Nabrit believed would soon be within reach. Harlan had written,

> *In the view of the Constitution, in the eye of the law, there is in this country no superior, dominant, ruling class of citizens. There is no caste here. Our Constitution is color-blind, and neither knows nor tolerates classes among its citizens. In respect of civil rights, all citizens are equal before the law. The humblest is the peer of the most powerful. The law regards man as man, and takes no account of his surroundings or of his color when his civil rights as guaranteed by the supreme law of the land are involved.*

Taking in the majesty and sweep of Harlan's words, Dovey resolved to spend her career fighting tirelessly against the lie of "separate but equal" expressed in the *Plessy* decision, for a justice system that made no distinction between rich and poor. She would work twice as hard if she had to.

Thanks to Nabrit's lectures, Dovey began to fully understand the power and potential of the Constitution. If properly interpreted, the document could be used to finally and firmly establish the civil rights of African Americans. She had once thought of Jim Crow as a solid, almost impenetrable barrier; now she saw that it stood on the shakiest of premises. Segregation, Nabrit told his students, opposed the Constitution's most sacred principles. Anything that is unconstitutional can never be legal.

Dovey:

> *James Nabrit was the one who made me a lawyer . . . Line by line, layer by layer, Dr. Nabrit ripped away the veneer of judicial authority that encased the* Plessy *decision, unmasking for us a truth that remained hidden from our privileged white counterparts at other law schools where, in the 1940s,* Plessy *was carefully ignored . . . Nabrit alone among American law professors had dared to take it on . . .*
>
> *Ours was a unique era for legal study, a time when it can truly be said that a single case held the key. If* Plessy v. Ferguson *could be dismantled, we stood to reshape America, to return it to the ideal of its origin, in a purer form. So long as it remained intact, justice eluded us.* Plessy *was a creation of the law, Nabrit told us repeatedly, and it could be undone by the law.*

While dismantling *Plessy* seemed logical enough during classroom discussions, it was much harder to accomplish in the nation's courtrooms. With seemingly favorable decisions leaving loopholes for southern states to exploit, victories were seldom complete. Black Americans cheered in 1946, when the Supreme Court handed down its ruling in

Morgan v. Virginia. Irene Morgan, a Black woman, had refused to move to the back of the bus while riding from Virginia to her Maryland home. In its decision, the court prohibited states from imposing their own Jim Crow restrictions on Black passengers traveling across state lines. The ruling, based on a clause in the Constitution about how commerce should be conducted across state lines, didn't address *Plessy* or the notion of "separate but equal." Still, it would make things easier for Black travelers. Or so it seemed. During Dovey's first year of law school, she had watched in horror as every single southern transit company reacted to *Morgan* by implementing its own rules separating passengers by race. Because they were private businesses, they were beyond the reach of the Supreme Court edict, which addressed state Jim Crow laws. The southern bus carriers made the most of that loophole.

Houston's army pressed on. Marshall, Nabrit, and their associates in the NAACP Legal Defense Fund (LDF) had also been challenging Jim Crow laws that confined Black children to substandard schools. Sitting in Nabrit's class, Dovey listened as he described the upcoming mission to focus such efforts on graduate and professional institutions. Vanquishing *Plessy* in higher education might make it easier to defeat in public schools, he explained.

In 1948, the Supreme Court had ruled in favor of Ada Lois Sipuel, a Black woman denied admission to the University of Oklahoma College of Law. School officials had told her she would have to defer her education until more African Americans applied. Then, they said, they would build a separate law school just for them. That made no sense to Sipuel. A legal team led by Thurgood Marshall took on her case. After a series of defeats in the state courts, they appealed to the US Supreme Court. When the court handed down its favorable decision, Dovey and the other members of her study group celebrated so loudly that the walls of her tiny apartment seemed to shake. But, as they discovered, it was too early to savor the victory.

Five days after the court's ruling was announced, Oklahoma officials roped off a corner of the state Capitol and pronounced it a new law school for African Americans. Sipuel refused to attend, and Marshall again appealed to the Supreme Court. Oklahoma's attorney general finally conceded, enabling Sipuel to enroll in 1949. As they had when roping off space for her in the Capitol building, the law school officials forced Lois Sipuel, who was by then married and expecting a child, to remain separate from white students in classrooms and common spaces. And the Supreme Court did nothing, at that point, to intervene.

Like the Morgan case before it, *Sipuel v. Board of Regents of the University of Oklahoma* had provided a hollow victory. While chipping away—slowly—at injustice, both cases left Jim Crow largely intact. The NAACP had been relying on a gradual approach for many years, arguing for improvement in separate facilities, classrooms, and vehicles without attacking "separate but equal" head-on. Dovey's favorite professor believed it was time for a change of strategy. Nabrit advised against allowing the court to suggest that establishing equal facilities for African Americans would make separation acceptable. Separation was never acceptable, he contended. It was un-American and unconstitutional. To avoid that fact was like tiptoeing around *Plessy* instead of confronting it directly. In the spring of 1950, Dovey's last semester of law school, Nabrit insisted it was time to face Jim Crow head-on.

Two critical upcoming cases offered Thurgood Marshall and his colleague Robert Carter the chance to employ the direct assault they'd been advocating. Both *McLaurin v. Oklahoma State Regents* and *Sweatt v. Painter* sought justice for Black plaintiffs denied access to higher education. Marshall and Carter rehearsed their arguments in mock trials held at Howard, with Nabrit acting as judge. Dovey and her classmates watched the preparations closely. Seeing these geniuses flex their legal muscles, she vowed to someday command a courtroom with equal flair.

One other case caught Dovey's eye as she planned for graduation. *Henderson v. United States et al.* was being argued by a brilliant Black attorney named Belford V. Lawson. The Yale-trained Lawson was not part of the NAACP team. He argued the case on behalf of Elmer Henderson, who had been a field representative for A. Philip Randolph's FEPC, just as Dovey had. His petition challenged a railway company for repeatedly denying him access to a crowded dining car during a trip from Washington, DC, to Birmingham, Alabama. Lawson's legal strategy included a frontal attack on *Plessy*, the same tactic Nabrit had called for.

On April 4, 1950, Lawson, like Marshall and Carter, argued his case before the Supreme Court. The same day, Dovey walked to Union Station to purchase two first-class train tickets for her mother and grandmother to travel to Washington on the Southern Railway to attend her graduation in May. Dovey had been working extra hours at a grocery store to earn enough money to pay their rail fare.

Civil rights plaintiff Elmer Henderson, who prevailed in the US Supreme Court in a 1950 Jim Crow complaint against Southern Railway.

Lela and Grandma Rachel had been unable to witness so many important moments in her life, including her graduation from Spelman and her wedding. She had vowed that she would let nothing stop them from seeing her graduate from Howard. The first-class tickets she had personally purchased would bypass Jim Crow laws. Or so she thought.

When she first spotted her mother and grandmother at the train station, she saw immediately that something was dreadfully wrong. Her grandmother was limping badly, and her mother was weeping. They could hardly hold on to their luggage. Dovey hurried across the crowded platform, sidestepping suitcases and dodging the elbows of scrambling passengers. She reached them just in time to prevent Rachel from collapsing to the ground.

"Grandma, what's wrong?" she asked. "Are you sick?"

"No, Dovey Mae. I ain't sick."

Rachel's voice was as soft as a whisper. She was too weak to talk, so Lela explained what had happened. The Jim Crow car had been so crowded that they had been forced to stand all the way from Charlotte to Washington—a ten-hour trip. With their "Reserved Seat" tickets in hand, they had tried to get to a half-empty car reserved for whites. Lela had hoped the conductor would note Rachel's advanced age and take pity on them. Instead, he'd threatened them, shouting until they retreated to the cramped, sweaty car from which they'd come. They passed through North Carolina, Virginia, and

Maryland—a journey of six hundred miles—managing to stay on their feet by gripping the backs of seats. Desperate and exhausted, seventy-five-year-old Rachel slumped atop a closed toilet in the bathroom and remained there until at last they reached Washington.

When Dovey examined her grandmother's feet in her apartment, she saw that they were so bruised and bloody that Dovey called a doctor. As a child, Dovey had eased her grandmother's pain by rubbing ointment into her aching feet, battered and disfigured by a white man who'd meant to assault her. Dovey was determined to help her grandmother again, but with legal knowledge and sound reasoning instead of turpentine and mutton tallow. Rachel was not permanently injured, a fact that provided no comfort to Dovey. Furious, she declared that she would sue Southern Railway, the same company named in Elmer Henderson's Supreme Court complaint. Belford Lawson had argued his case as a sole practitioner, without assistance or money from the NAACP. If he could pursue justice on his own, perhaps she could as well. She thought of little else, even as the days rushed past and she marched into the campus chapel to receive her diploma. The court ruled in Henderson's favor a week after Lela and Rachel returned to Charlotte.

The court's decision made no mention of the constitutional questions Lawson had raised. Still, it condemned the carrier's treatment of Henderson as unreasonable and unfair. The ruling wasn't quite a rejection of *Plessy*, but it was enough to encourage Dovey in her own conflict with Southern Railway. She had no desire to subject her elderly grandmother to the rigors of a trial. A monetary damage award, however, seemed within the range of possibility. Dovey had not yet been admitted to the bar of the District of Columbia, but her classmate and ally, Julius Robertson, had, and the two of them were planning to go into practice together. She asked Julius to file a breach-of-contract complaint in the US District Court for the District of Columbia on behalf of her mother and grandmother.

The case proceeded slowly and included the railway attorney's visits to Charlotte to take depositions from Lela and Rachel. Nearly a year passed. Dovey had been sworn in to the DC bar and was officially a professional attorney. She was still getting accustomed to her new responsibilities when Southern Railway offered a settlement of several hundred dollars. Dovey was deeply disappointed. Accepting Julius's advice, she agreed to the offer. But her dissatisfaction lingered. After all, no amount of money could compensate for her family's pain and suffering. In contrast, the railway wouldn't suffer at all. The company would pay nothing for its cruelty besides a few pennies. It could write a check and be done with the matter, continuing to discriminate and humiliate African Americans as it had always done. Dovey knew, of course, that it wasn't merely the railway that deserved her anger; it was the entire system that sustained it. The country had long ignored the Thirteenth, Fourteenth, and Fifteenth Amendments, clinging instead to the outdated perspective of *Plessy v. Ferguson*. As a result, families like hers continued to be stuck in second-class citizenship no matter how hard they worked, no matter how much they studied.

Dovey:

> *And so the system that had reduced my folk to subhuman status rolled onward, untouched. And the country that permitted it, the America that had long ago breached its contract with its citizens, remained unchanged.*

The system remained unchanged, but there was one important difference: Dovey Johnson Roundtree was a licensed attorney now. She was ready, willing, and able to fight.

Dovey Johnson Roundtree on the occasion of her graduation from Howard University School of Law, 1950.

Lela Johnson and Rachel Bryant Graham, circa 1950.

CHAPTER 6

IN PURSUIT OF JUSTICE

The last time Dovey had listened to Professor James Nabrit lecture, she'd been a third-year law student. Now here she was again, on Howard's campus, sitting spellbound while Nabrit shared his wisdom. It was April 1952, less than a year after Dovey had passed the bar exam that enabled her to practice in the nation's capital. Four cases challenging segregation in public schools were heading toward the US Supreme Court. Nabrit had invited more than two hundred lawyers, scholars, and journalists to the law school, seeking agreement on the best way to present the cases, known collectively as *Brown v. Board of Education.* To Dovey's delight and astonishment, Nabrit had chosen to include her.

It was nearly two years to the day since Charles Hamilton

Houston had died of a heart attack. Nabrit stepped in to lead his last case, *Bolling v. Sharpe*, a public school desegregation case. He had just taken it to the US Court of Appeals for the District of Columbia Circuit. Depending on the outcome there, the case might move forward to the Supreme Court along with the four state cases Thurgood Marshall and the rest of the NAACP Legal Defense Fund team were preparing to argue in the high court.

Within the ranks of the LDF lawyers, there was sharp disagreement about the best approach to take, whether to continue the careful, tempered path of past years or to launch a direct hit on segregation. At the Howard gathering, Dovey watched Nabrit tear into supporters of a tempered approach. "The attack should be waged with the most devastating forces at hand," he said, his voice ringing out across the auditorium. "Instead of worrying over the effect of compelling the court to decide, our real concern is how we may best compel the Supreme Court to decide the question. Let the Supreme Court take the blame if it dares to say to the entire world, '*Yes*, democracy rests on a legalized caste system. Segregation of the races is legal.' Make the court choose. Let the court make a national and international record of this. Let the court write this across the face of the Constitution: 'All men are equal, but white men are more equal than others.'"

Nabrit's words stayed in Dovey's head long after the assembly had ended, even as she and Julius Robertson worked to establish their partnership. The tiny firm of Robertson and Roundtree eventually settled into a rented office at 1931 Eleventh Street, Northwest. Both partners continued to hold down other jobs while building their practice. Julius supported his wife and four children by working nights at the post office. Dovey worked days as an attorney-adviser reviewing contracts for the Labor Department. She was a pioneer in her field, one of a handful of Black women practicing law in the District of Columbia, following proudly in the footsteps of her law school mentor Ollie Mae Cooper. The pair worked around the clock, never forgetting Charles Hamilton Houston's dictum that a Black lawyer must always seek justice. To do otherwise, he'd said, was to be a "parasite on society."

In the streets and courtrooms of Washington, Black attorneys faced the same problems that their clients wrestled with. They had to leave the courthouse for bathroom breaks and meals gulped down between cases. And the odds were stacked against them inside the courtrooms as well, where they faced white judges who were generally hostile to them. African American clients hesitated to hire Black lawyers, for fear they would not get a fair hearing. Despite the difficulties, the nation's capital had a small, ambitious group of Black attorneys, some of them seasoned veterans of the struggle for justice. Excited to join their community, Dovey and Julius took every case that came their way. Like Dovey,

Julius believed in the value of family ties, and his commitment to justice matched her own. On top of all that, he was a loyal protector who had earned her trust.

Some clients, referred to them by the NAACP, took a bold stand in the face of injustice. One of their first cases involved a man named Walter J. Leonard, who chose to testify against a policeman who had beaten an unarmed man. Leonard became a protégé of Dovey's, attending Howard Law School and eventually becoming an associate dean of Harvard Law. Astute and unflinching, Leonard took a risk few Blacks in that period would have braved.

Other clients were ordinary people in trouble. In segregated Washington, trouble lurked everywhere. Something as simple as a moving violation or a mistaken glance could land a Black citizen on the wrong side of the law. Business began to pick up when a respected member of Dovey's church enlisted her help in arranging a last will and testament. The client wanted to make sure that her belongings were passed on to the proper recipients after her death. When Dovey performed to her new client's satisfaction, word of her talent began to spread. Soon she and Julius were handling wills for clients all over southeast Washington. When people were unable to pay them in cash, the partners were happy to accept other goods in exchange for their services. On one occasion, they arrived at work to find a basket from a satisfied client sitting on the doorstep. Inside were eggs, collard greens, and peppers. Sometimes green vegetables were just as good as green dollars.

Soon after starting her practice, Dovey paid a visit to Dr. Bethune. The National Council of Negro Women had continued to prosper under her leadership during Dovey's law school years. The NCNW now occupied an imposing three-story Victorian in northwest Washington. Dovey climbed the steps to Bethune's third-floor office and presented her with an offer: She would provide legal service to the council. Free of charge. For the rest of her life. It would add to the duties that her practice already imposed, but in Dovey's view, it was the least she could do for a woman who had done so much for her. As she left and headed back to her own office, she allowed herself a small moment of satisfaction. She had followed Miss Neptune's advice by doing more than paying back what she owed. She was acknowledging an act of kindness and passing it on.

For nearly as long as trains and streetcars and buses had existed in the United States, there had been laws and customs segregating them by race. For as long as those restrictions had existed, there had been Black women rebelling against them. The great journalist Ida B. Wells, ejected from a whites-only railway car in 1884, sued and won, only to have the ruling overturned on appeal. Dovey's ordeal on a Miami bus had taken place in 1943. Three years later, Irene Morgan, who had refused to move to the back of a Virginia bus, had won a hollow victory in the Supreme Court, whose ruling in her favor was dodged by all the southern bus companies.

There would be more women to come in the near future, including Aurelia Browder, Susie McDonald, Claudette Colvin, Mary Louise Smith, and Rosa Parks. In 1955, all of them would be arrested for violating bus segregation laws in Montgomery, Alabama, and Rosa Parks would become a national symbol of defiance of Jim Crow. The bus boycott that followed their arrests, led by Rev. Martin Luther King Jr., drew the eyes of the entire country to the South, its Jim Crow laws, and its violent methods of enforcing them. With King leading the charge, Black men and women all over the South, and many from the North, would take on segregation in the streets, in the churches, everywhere Jim Crow prevailed.

But that day was still three years into the

African American women walking to work during the yearlong Montgomery Bus Boycott.

future when Private First Class Sarah Louise Keys arrived at the door of Dovey and Julius's law office on a September afternoon in 1952. Quiet and shy, Sarah Keys didn't look as though she belonged in the same bold company of such women as Ida B. Wells or Irene Morgan. But like Rosa Parks, Sarah Keys would become a crucial soldier in the battle for civil rights.

Accompanied by her father, she arrived at the office of Robertson and Roundtree dressed in a crisply starched army uniform and cap. She said little at first, content to let her father tell her story of mistreatment on a North Carolina bus. David Keys, a farmer and stonemason, had exhausted his resources in North Carolina, so the local NAACP had referred him to its Washington office. When Sarah finally spoke, she talked so softly that Dovey and Julius had to lean forward to hear her.

On the morning of August 1, she'd risen early and boarded a Safeway Trails bus. About to enjoy her first furlough since enlisting, she'd left Fort Dix in New Jersey to return to her hometown of Washington, North Carolina, wearing her uniform for the trip.

She'd traveled without incident to Washington, DC, where she transferred to a bus that would take her the rest of the way. She found a seat in the fifth row from the front and, lulled by the rhythm of rubber hitting road, soon fell asleep. A rude voice awakened her, and she opened her eyes to discover that the bus had come to a stop in a little town called Roanoke Rapids, North Carolina, and that a different driver had taken over the route. He told her to give up her seat to a white marine and find a spot in the back.

"I told him I preferred to stay where I was," Sarah recalled, her voice growing in volume and power. Listening to her, Dovey resisted the urge to shake her head in frustration. It had been six years since *Morgan v. Virginia*, a ruling that African Americans had celebrated. They were anticipating change that never came. Private companies, exempt from laws regulating states, imposed their own segregationist rules. They enabled

A Black passenger in Durham, North Carolina, 1940, standing beneath a "Colored Waiting Room" sign opposite a Carolina Coach bus.

conductors and drivers to humiliate and harass Black passengers like Sarah Keys whenever they pleased.

Her driver ordered everyone off the bus except her. She got off anyway and followed the driver as he led the other passengers to a nearby bus, its motor already running. He slammed the doors in her face and took off. It was after midnight, and Sarah was all alone in the little town of Roanoke Rapids. She went into the station looking for help, but all she got was hostility. The ticket clerk and the dispatcher said nothing, looking right through her as if she weren't there. Desperate and growing more afraid, she ran to a policeman. "I showed him my ticket and explained I needed to get home. He told me, 'You shut up before we have to take you down and lock you up.'"

Before she knew it, the police officer was forcing her from the station and shoving her into his squad car. He told her she was under arrest for disorderly conduct. "If you say one more word," he warned, "I'll slap you across the face."

Sarah had wound up in jail, with no way to contact her parents or anyone else. Few lawyers could have related to her experience as intimately as Dovey. Nine years earlier, she, too, had been tossed from a bus while wearing her military uniform, stranded in darkness in an unfamiliar place. Earlier than that, while still at Spelman, she had known the terror of confinement in a jail cell, separated from loved ones and anyone else who could help her. While listening to Sarah,

Dovey felt the years fall away in a single moment. She knew that the young private must have felt frightened, desperate, and alone. "It was as though I sat looking in a mirror, so strong was my sense of having walked where Sarah Keys had walked," Dovey later said.

Sarah had stayed behind bars until morning, when the local mayor held a quick trial and immediately pronounced her guilty of disorderly conduct.

Sarah finished her story, with her father flinching at each familiar detail. Dovey and Julius looked at each other, knowing that they would agree to take up her cause. Their friendship, begun during Dovey's first days in law school, had strengthened during the days and countless study sessions that followed, to the extent that they generally read each other's thoughts when it came to legal matters.

They told Sarah about all the hurdles in front of them. She would face hard questioning. The case would take a long time, maybe years. It might not lead to anything good. Sarah assured them she would see it through, no matter the cost. Dovey and Julius smiled. Nothing about Sarah's demure appearance had suggested she would be a rebel. But a rebel she was.

Dovey couldn't afford to leave her job at the Department of Labor, nor could Julius give up his work at the post office. Still, both knew that *Sarah Keys v. Carolina Coach Company* would require long hours of preparation. They went at it with all they had, devoting every spare hour to examining the case from all angles. Finally they came up with an opening strategy: a claim of breach of contract. The northern carrier, Safeway Trails, had sold Sarah a ticket providing for uninterrupted transport from Trenton, New Jersey, to Washington, North Carolina. The ticket was, in essence, a contract. The bus company had violated it by failing to carry her all the way home.

Dovey had tried a similar tactic in the case involving her mother and grandmother. This time she and Julius planned to use the same method Belford Lawson had employed in *Henderson v. United States et al.* The wily courtroom veteran, whose office was right across the street from Robertson and Roundtree's, had cited a law called the Interstate Commerce Act, which regulated trade and travel across state lines. The act prohibited what it called "undue and unreasonable prejudice," the kind of treatment Lawson argued his client, Elmer Henderson, had been subjected to on Southern Railway. Dovey and Julius viewed Sarah Keys's treatment in exactly the same way.

Meanwhile, the battle on the education front continued. The NAACP Legal Defense Fund no longer planned to address unequal conditions found in Black schools. Their new strategy reflected what Nabrit had been advocating for years: They would argue that segregation under any circumstances is wrong, is harmful to children, and is a denial of the equal protection provided to them under the Fourteenth Amendment.

Dovey, Julius, and every lawyer they knew breathlessly awaited the upcoming proceedings. They all wondered the same thing: Would the court undermine *Plessy* by restoring the Fourteenth Amendment to its full strength?

A little-known railway segregation case called *Mitchell v. United States* had helped pave the way. Arthur Mitchell, a lawyer and the first Black person in history elected to Congress as a Democrat, filed suit after being forced to sit in a segregated railway car while traveling from Chicago to Arkansas. In March 1941, he brought his case before the US Supreme Court. On April 28, the court decided in his favor. Writing the unanimous opinion, Chief Justice Charles Evan Hughes noted, "The denial to appellant of equality of accommodations because of his race would be an invasion of a fundamental individual right which is guaranteed against state action by the Fourteenth Amendment." Dovey and Julius planned to make a similar argument in the case of Sarah Louise Keys.

In November, they sued on the basis of four counts:

1. Breach of contract.
2. Violation of the Interstate Commerce Act's ban on "unreasonable prejudice."
3. False arrest, violating Sarah's right to equal treatment under the Fourteenth Amendment.
4. Mental anguish caused by Sarah's ordeal.

They asked for $10,000 per count and petitioned to have a jury trial held in the federal district court in the District of Columbia.

That same week, James Nabrit successfully petitioned to have *Bolling v. Sharpe*, his District of Columbia school-segregation case, heard at the Supreme Court with the four public school cases. Oral arguments would be presented on December 9, 1952.

When that date rolled around, Thurgood Marshall began the proceedings by arguing *Briggs v. Elliott*, the South Carolina case. In the gallery, Dovey and Julius had front-row seats. Nabrit had rewarded two of his best students with day passes granting them admission. Dovey hardly blinked as the judges emerged from behind the velvet curtain. She listened intently as Marshall, tall and charming, laid out the merits of his case. Again and again, he returned to the Fourteenth Amendment as a protector of all citizens, including little Black schoolchildren who just wanted a good education. If Marshall prevailed, African Americans would be one step closer to seeing *Plessy v. Ferguson* overturned. Dovey and Julius followed his arguments closely, searching for ideas and methods that might help their own case.

When she returned to her office, her joy at witnessing Marshall's historic brilliance evaporated. She and Julius learned that Carolina Trailways had refused their summons.

The company had been responsible for the southern part of Sarah's journey, from Washington, DC, to Washington, North Carolina. Its lawyers argued that because it was a Virginia-based company, it could not be sued in a District of Columbia court. While the partners scrambled to find a solution, the company that had handled the northern part of Sarah's trip also refused her claim. Lawyers for Safeway Trails contended that the company had no obligations beyond getting passengers safely to Washington, DC. Anything that happened to them farther south was beyond the bus company's control. The US District Court for the District of Columbia upheld the carrier's argument. On February 23, 1953, it dismissed the case on the basis that the District of Columbia had no jurisdiction.

Although Sarah was crushed, Dovey quickly recovered. At Howard she had learned that any struggle worth fighting for was bound to have a few setbacks and reversals. Besides, she had warned Sarah from the beginning that they would face serious challenges. The dismissal meant the courts were no longer an option. She and Julius realized that to find any path to justice in the case, they would have to face an administrative agency they had hoped to avoid: the Interstate Commerce Commission (ICC). Its job was to enforce the Interstate Commerce Act, the law governing modes of transportation between states.

The Interstate Commerce Act forbade "unjust and unreasonable prejudice" against all passengers. But in the sixty-six years of its existence, the ICC had taken the position that segregation of Black passengers on buses and trains was not a form of discrimination. Like the Supreme Court in *Plessy*, the commission said that separate facilities were in fact equal. On the few occasions that African American train travelers had protested this interpretation, the ICC had ruled against them. And no Black bus traveler had ever brought a case before the ICC.

The odds were steep, but the partners pressed on. The fact that the Supreme Court was preparing to hear the public

THE INTERSTATE COMMERCE COMMISSION:
A Reluctant Player in the Fight for Civil Rights

When most people think of the legal fight for civil rights, the Supreme Court is the battleground that comes to mind, with the Fourteenth Amendment as the main piece of ammunition. However, the Supreme Court and the Fourteenth Amendment were not the only important elements in the war for civil rights. In 1887, Congress passed the **Interstate Commerce Act** to prevent unfair discrimination in railway rates, and the act created an agency, the **Interstate Commerce Commission** (ICC), to enforce its provisions. The ICC, like the many other federal agencies that were formed after it—the Federal Trade Commission and the Food and Drug Administration, for example—had significant powers of enforcement even though it was not technically a court. The ICC's job was to regulate commerce—that is, trade and business—among the states by enforcing the rules of the Interstate Commerce Act. One of those rules forbade bus and train companies that crossed state lines from subjecting passengers to "unjust discrimination" and "undue and unreasonable prejudice." When Congress passed the act in 1887, it meant to prevent the powerful and wealthy railway companies from discriminating against poor rural passengers, especially farmers, with high fares they could never hope to afford. They hadn't been thinking of Black travelers at all. Yet, as Jim Crow laws expanded school desegregation cases gave them hope. And a victory before the ICC would be a monumental breakthrough, given the power the commission wielded. The ICC was the agency charged with putting up—or taking down—the hated WHITES ONLY or COLORED signs on trains and buses.

To win a favorable order from the ICC had the potential to change life for Black travelers all over the South. Dovey and Julius quit their outside jobs and devoted themselves full-time to the pursuit of justice.

On September 1, 1953, Sarah petitioned the ICC. She was the first Black passenger ever to file a complaint specifically about bus travel. Three months later, the Supreme

across the South, African American travelers began looking to the words of the Interstate Commerce Act to protect them from the unfairness of segregation.

For many years, they got nowhere. The ICC held strictly to the policy of "separate but equal"—which the Supreme Court had put in place with the notorious 1896 case of *Plessy v. Ferguson*. The commission took the position that so long as the facilities for Black travelers were substantially equal to those for whites, the separation of the races was not "unjust discrimination." In the 1930s and '40s, the commission ruled against every African American who filed a Jim Crow complaint. Not even the Supreme Court's 1946 ruling in *Morgan v. Virginia*, banning states from imposing their Jim Crow laws on interstate buses, swayed the ICC's ironclad segregation policy.

The Interstate Commerce Commission was dissolved in 1995, and most of its functions were taken over by a new agency called the Surface Transportation Board. At the time the commission was abolished, the National Archives chose to preserve only the ICC's train cases. All its bus case files, including *Keys*, were shredded. Portions of the *Keys* case file are available in the Department of Justice collection in the National Archives and in the papers of Robert F. Kennedy, housed at the John F. Kennedy Presidential Library in Boston.

A Black air force officer, 1956, outside a segregated waiting room in an Atlanta bus station.

Court heard a second round of arguments in the *Brown* cases. Dovey and Julius watched carefully. If the Supreme Court took arguments about the equal protection clause seriously, perhaps the ICC would feel compelled to do the same.

Five days after a tough hearing in which an attorney for Carolina Trailways grilled Sarah relentlessly, the Supreme Court ruled on *Brown*. Dovey and Julius, guests of James Nabrit, were in the chambers when Chief Justice Earl Warren read the court's unanimous opinion. Does segregation of children in public schools solely on the basis of race harm children, he asked, even if the schools are otherwise equal?

Dovey sighed and closed her eyes as Warren answered his own question: "We believe that it does." Dovey's relief turned to outright joy as the chief justice continued to dismantle *Plessy*. He went on to affirm that segregation violated the equal protection clause of the Fourteenth Amendment. Seven years earlier, Charles Hamilton Houston had issued that rallying cry: "There is no such thing as separate but equal." And now Chief Justice Earl Warren echoed his words. "We conclude unanimously," he said,

NAACP Legal Defense Fund attorneys (from left) George E. C. Hayes, Thurgood Marshall, and James Nabrit outside the Supreme Court after their May 17, 1954, victory in the landmark school desegregation ruling *Brown v. Board of Education*.

"that in the field of public education the doctrine of 'separate but equal' has no place."

Dovey:

> As Warren moved forward to take Plessy head on, I felt the ugliness that had shadowed my life from childhood draining away. The cuts and the hurts and the signs, the words of the trolley car driver in Charlotte, the shouts of army officers separating me from my fellow officers, the terror of the night in the Miami bus station—all of it evaporated.
>
> I felt as though I was being born again. I was being born again, and so was every other Black person in America.

CHAPTER 7

ROBERTSON AND ROUNDTREE

A week later, the US Supreme Court struck down segregation in golf courses, public housing, and amusement parks. When Chief Justice Warren had announced the *Brown* ruling, he'd declared that Jim Crow had no place in public education. Now it seemed unwelcome anywhere, at least for the moment.

At the law office of Robertson and Roundtree at 1931 Eleventh Street NW, the partners viewed the new announcements as favorable developments for the *Keys* case. The Supreme Court had handed down what sounded like a mandate for the entire country, including the Interstate Commerce Commission. Dovey hoped Isadore Freidson, the ICC examiner, would see things the same way.

He did not. September 30, 1954, a letter from Freidson arrived. He concluded that Carolina Coach Company had not subjected Sarah Keys "to any unjust discrimination or undue and unreasonable prejudice or disadvantage." Therefore, he contended, Sarah's complaint should be dismissed. Adding insult to injury, Freidson explained that *Brown* did not apply to private businesses such as bus companies. He wrote, "The recent rejection by the Supreme Court, in respect to the issue of public education . . . in no way affects or prohibits separation or segregation of the Negro and white races insofar as transportation is concerned."

The ICC examiner wasn't pretending that *Brown* had never happened. He was just insisting that it didn't matter.

Dovey had long known better than to count on a favorable outcome in any legal matter. When she was in law school, her professors had stressed the importance of taking nothing for granted. Still, she was stunned and frustrated by Freidson's letter. She went to see James Nabrit and told him how she felt. Years before, when she had been a headstrong undergraduate raging at injustice, Miss Neptune had assured her that a new day would indeed come—but first she had to set aside the anger that hindered her. In the wake of Freidson's decision, Nabrit told her nearly the same thing. He said that her rage was understandable but that it wouldn't help her in the long run. "You have to move past your anger," he advised, "or it will consume you." While Dovey struggled to cool her temper,

she worked with Julius to file an exception with the ICC. They
had just twenty days to appeal Freidson's ruling before it took
on the force of law. The last round of arguments had involved
a hearing with just one examiner. For the next one, they'd
make their case to all eleven commissioners.

By then the partners had been working on *Keys* for two
years. At first, they had set aside hours whenever possible,
spending early mornings and late afternoons mapping out a
preliminary strategy. In 1953 they'd finally quit their other
jobs to focus full-time on their practice. Outside the office,
they'd camped out in the Howard Law School library, sift-
ing through past cases of transportation law as if they were
still students tackling Professor Nabrit's massive reading list.
They'd followed the developments in the five school cases,
paying close attention to the issues connecting them to *Keys*.
All the while, Julius had made sure Dovey gained valuable
experience trying cases before judges and juries.

Their new brief argued that allowing private buses to
devise their own seating regulations was not only unjust
but also a recipe for chaos. Conflicting policies made interstate travel so confusing that states were prohibited from
enacting their own travel laws; why were private companies granted that right? They went on to cite a number of
earlier cases that supported their arguments against racial
discrimination. Finally they took direct aim at examiner Isadore Freidson's casual dismissal of *Brown*. In any

reasonable interaction, they wrote, "it is logical to assert" that the Supreme Court's prohibition of segregation in public schools could be expanded to "fields affected with a public interest," including buses.

Dovey:

> We were demanding that the commission do what they'd resisted doing for the sixty-six years of their existence. They must, we asserted, protect the rights of travelers as much as they did the rights of the conveyances upon which they traveled. They must condemn the conduct of drivers who isolated and bullied passengers for no other reason than the color of their skin. They must declare that segregation, standing alone, amounted to unjust discrimination and unreasonable prejudice against Sarah Keys and members of her race, and that such discrimination and prejudice worked to the disadvantage of any Negro traveler.

Dovey and Julius filed the exception on October 19, 1954, one day before the deadline. They had cautioned their client that the pace of law could be agonizingly slow. Sarah would find that they hadn't exaggerated. The ICC waited more than a year before responding.

Its answer arrived quietly, in a brown envelope. But when Dovey and Julius read it, they felt as though the commission had shouted its decision from the rooftops: It was such a radical departure from its long segregationist history. The ICC ruled in the matter of *Keys v. Carolina Coach Company* and in a companion case, *NAACP v. St. Louis–San Francisco Railway Company*. At long last, the so-called Supreme Court of the Confederacy interpreted the Interstate Commerce Act as a prohibition on segregation itself. The commission declared:

"We conclude that the assignment of seats in interstate buses, so designated as to imply the inherent inferiority of a traveler solely because of race or color, must be regarded as subjecting the traveler to unjust discrimination, and undue and unreasonable prejudice and disadvantage."

Sarah's long wait was over. She had won.

After sixty-six years of supporting Jim Crow, the ICC had finally spoken out, just as the Supreme Court had, for racial justice.

The ruling covered more ground than Dovey had dared to dream of. Going beyond buses and trains, the ICC's language appeared to imply that segregation in the stations and waiting rooms also violated the Interstate Commerce Act. Only restaurants in the bus and train terminals were not affected by the new regulations. As private businesses, they continued to be exempt. The ICC issued its orders on November 25, 1955, just a week before Rosa Parks's arrest in Mongomery. The commission's ruling ordered that Jim Crow and all its ropes, borders, and signs be removed by January 10, 1956.

But the bus companies that traveled throughout the South were not about to comply. They threatened litigation against the ICC, or simple noncompliance. And it became clear, in the aftermath of the ruling, that the commission itself was not going to take on the task of enforcing its own ruling. There had been one lone dissenter in the *Keys* opinion, a South Carolina Democrat named J. Monroe Johnson, and shortly after the ruling was issued, Johnson advanced to the chairmanship of the ICC. He saw to it that the *Keys* ruling remained unenforced, that the ugliness of Jim Crow on southern buses persisted.

While the decision in *Keys v. Carolina Coach Company* lay buried in the Interstate Commerce Commission offices in Washington, another campaign of the civil rights movement was taking shape—a campaign that would explode in southern cities, bus terminals, and lunch counters with such force that all of America took notice.

It would take six years, two more rulings by the Supreme Court concerning bus travel, and a protest by the group of activists known as the Freedom Riders to bring about the change that the *Keys* case had promised.

Dovey:

In the six years that separated Keys from the day in September 1961 when the ICC finally acted in accordance with the order it had issued in 1955, I . . . became a different person, a different sort of lawyer, in fact, from the one who'd battled the ICC. I am not sure that I chose that path, so much as it chose me.

People chose me, people in real pain. And there were hundreds of them in the District of Columbia, more than I'd ever imagined until I started practicing law . . . To our doorstep came clients who were hurting in every way human beings can hurt—mothers fighting for their children, fathers fighting for their jobs, teenagers who'd been preyed upon by the adults charged with their care, husbands and wives in bitter custody battles, victims of violent crimes.

Julius, for his part, fought the civil rights battle on the ground with the magazine he had founded, called *Stride*, in which he published articles on politics, business, and law. A stream of clients poured through their office doors. And new clients weren't the only people to converge on their offices. Black attorneys started showing up as well, with questions.

Dovey:

We'd proven something every Black lawyer had wanted to believe, and now could: that we had a fair shot at winning damage awards before white judges, if we worked the cases expertly enough. Our colleagues began phoning for advice, and Julius and I began holding after-hours seminars on personal injury law. The office became a hub for a new generation of Black lawyers eager to prove the old way wrong.

Dovey Johnson Roundtree, circa 1960–65, during the period when she argued her most famous criminal case, *US v. Ray Crump.*

Dovey found that she loved teaching law and loved mentoring younger lawyers even more. At the age of forty-five, she'd taken up the mantle of professors she'd admired, men like James Nabrit and George Hayes.

Between trying cases, filing suits, and conducting after-hours study sessions in her office, she had little opportunity to rest. By the end of 1958, she had taken ill. Diabetes and tumors left her underweight and weak. Believing she didn't have time to be sick, she refused to consider reducing her caseload. Nor would she seek assistance from Julius. With his court schedule, his magazine, and his family responsibilities, he was also working too hard for his own good. Her solution was to keep rushing. Racing came as naturally to her as breathing, after all. Hadn't she sprinted across Spelman's campus so swiftly that the school president had warned her to learn to "walk like a Spelman woman"? Hadn't she hurried from trial to trial, served on church committees, and fulfilled speaking engagements day after day?

It all caught up with her in the early months of 1959. She became so sick that friends rushed her to the hospital, where she underwent emergency surgery to remove the tumors. During her two weeks of recovery, she lay in her hospital bed, contemplating her future. For some time she had felt a certain restlessness that she couldn't shake. She had endured bouts of restlessness throughout her life. But nothing had been able to solve it this time, not even prayer. Finally, with a pastor friend visiting at her bedside, she arrived at a realization. "What would you say," she asked him, "if I told you I wanted to become a minister?" Her own words astonished her.

Women had few opportunities in the African Methodist Episcopal denomination to which Dovey belonged. They could preach in their local churches, but they weren't permitted to serve as "itinerant ministers" who could pastor, bestow blessings, administer communion, and officiate at funerals and weddings. Only men could do that. Despite those limitations, Rev. Charles Green, a friend of Dovey's who pastored at Pilgrim Baptist Church in southeast Washington, responded enthusiastically to Dovey's question. He told her that he'd seen the way audiences responded to her, that she'd touched people with her speeches. But there would be hurdles.

"People will not readily accept this lawyer who is a preacher, this preacher who is a lawyer," he said. "You must think further and pray. And if, then, you are determined to go forward, I am in it with you, all the way. We'll go over to Howard, to the divinity school. I'll have you meet all the great folk I know over there, and we'll get this going."

After leaving the hospital, Dovey headed home to Charlotte for more rest and recovery. Grandma Rachel, even at eighty-five, ran her household just as she had when Dovey was a little girl. She insisted now on cooking Dovey's favorite meals, filling the air with tantalizing scents. After two days in Rachel's care, Dovey told her grandmother about her desire to preach. They were alone on the screened porch when she confessed her feelings. The older woman said nothing for several long minutes. Instead, she looked into her granddaughter's eyes with a steady gaze. "Well, child," she said at last, "if you don't preach, you will die."

Rachel turned and left the porch, leaving Dovey to ponder her words in silence.

Dovey:

> *It would be years before I fully grasped the depth of her wisdom. In the moment, I was crushed. In fact, I cried afterward, standing alone there, I was so stung by her abruptness. I had wanted, in my naivete, an outburst of enthusiastic support, a hug, a few words of encouragement. But Grandma had understood as I had not, then, that any display of emotion would have belittled what God had ordained, and that when we tread on sacred ground, we gravely imperil ourselves.*

After obtaining her mother's blessing as well, Dovey returned to Washington and enrolled in night classes at Howard, studying scripture and theology. As her restlessness faded, she regained the peaceful feelings that had once eluded her. She still wanted to heal the world; she simply had found yet another way to do it. By day, she continued to practice law, toiling alongside Julius amid stacks of cases. Robertson and Roundtree continued to thrive, even as the surrounding world became increasingly torn apart by the civil rights struggle.

In January 1960, the Supreme Court handed down its ruling in an important bus desegregation case called *Boynton v. Virginia*. Whereas the *Keys* case had left eating facilities alone while banning Jim Crow on the trains and buses and in terminals, *Boynton* went further by prohibiting segregation at the lunch counters and soda fountains that serviced the passengers. The southern states immediately announced their refusal to comply with the court's desegregation order, just as they had done when the ICC handed down the *Keys* ruling. But this time, armies of civil rights activists stood ready to take the battle to the streets. In the years since *Keys*, the Reverend Martin Luther King Jr. had risen to national prominence in the wake of the Montgomery Bus Boycott, and organizations such as the Student Nonviolent Coordinating Committee (SNCC) and the Congress of Racial Equality (CORE) had begun launching boycotts, sit-ins, marches, and protests.

In May 1961, CORE leaders organized a group of Black and white activists called Freedom Riders to test the Supreme Court's ruling in the *Boynton* case, as well as the 1946 ruling in *Morgan v. Virginia*. They boarded buses in the North and rode together into the South, insisting on equal service everywhere they went. Theirs was a strategy of nonviolence. When white mobs confronted them in Montgomery, spilling blood and creating mayhem, the Freedom Riders responded only with passive resistance. They knew to expect violence, that the white crowds would be enraged at the sight of them disrupting the status quo on desegregated buses. The local police cooperated with the Ku Klux Klan by allowing the Klansmen to attack the bus passengers as they disembarked. John Lewis, one of the Freedom Riders, was twenty years old at the time. He recalled that "men, women, children, and teenagers . . . started beating people with anything they could use as a weapon. We thought we were going to die on that day."

On May 14, 1961, members of the Ku Klux Klan set one of the Freedom Riders' buses aflame outside a little Alabama town named Anniston. Television footage and newspaper reports of the violence shocked and horrified Americans across the country. At first, Attorney General Robert F. Kennedy had questioned the wisdom of the activists' knowingly riding into danger. But the whole world watched the television footage of white mobs beating the Freedom Riders on the platforms of southern bus terminals. Secretary of State Dean Rusk wrote a letter to Attorney General Kennedy, telling him that what was happening in the southern bus stations was embarrassing the United States in the eyes of the

In an image shown around the world, activists on a Freedom Ride sit outside a Greyhound bus set afire by white mobs outside Anniston, Alabama, on May 14, 1961.

entire world. Kennedy was moved to action. His team of lawyers at the Department of Justice swung into action. But they needed ammunition.

For years, the Interstate Commerce Commission, which was responsible for putting up and taking down the segregation signs, had refused to act—openly defying the Supreme Court. But the ICC could not deny its own words in *Keys v. Carolina Coach Company*. The case became Kennedy's ammunition. In an unusual legal document, Robert Kennedy's lawyers sent a petition to the ICC, demanding that it enforce its own ruling, quoting from the case the ICC's own words, the words that Julius and Dovey had wrung from the commission in 1955. Cornered by its own ruling, the commission quickly gave in to the attorney general's demands. It banned segregation everywhere within its jurisdiction, giving trains, buses, terminals, and restaurants six weeks to comply. At long last, the hated WHITES ONLY and COLORED signs came down—by order of the ICC.

"The smallest case can bellow in its own good time," Dovey said of the *Keys* case years later. Silent and unrecognized for six years, it armed Attorney General Kennedy at a critical moment in history. It bellowed.

Dovey and Julius celebrated as they watched their labor bear fruit. If anyone had told Dovey in 1952 that one of her quietest battles would wind its way into the very center of the civil rights movement in 1961, that it would embolden the nation's attorney general to *finally* bring segregated buses to an end, she would not have believed it. Change had finally come, and it was about time.

However, their victory left little time for rejoicing. As always, there were other cases to prepare, problems to solve, people to help. Their court calendar was often booked with trials back-to-back. Amid ringing phones, the bustle of office work, and the coming and going of clients, Dovey and Julius worried about each other's health. But neither of them could slow down.

In November, Julius was admitted to the hospital with chest pains. He'd been stricken in court, and Dovey had hoped the experience would finally persuade him to stop working so hard. But the recognition came too late. He died in the night, before Dovey could say goodbye.

Somehow, Julius had seen in Dovey talents and gifts she couldn't see in herself. From the beginning, he saw in her the accomplished attorney she was destined to become. He was a mentor among mentors, a man with the rare ability to relate to a woman as a peer and trusted confidante. Always, he was concerned that his colleagues accord Dovey equal status with him. He rushed to reassure her when he saw her reacting to someone's suggestion that perhaps she had no business trying cases. "It makes no difference that you're a woman, DJ," he'd say, smiling and shaking his head. "You're a damned good lawyer!"

Dovey had lost her friend and ally, her partner. Robertson and Roundtree was no more.

CHAPTER 8

GOING IT ALONE

Dovey grieved hard after the death of her friend and partner in 1961. Julius's demise was the first in a series of losses she suffered during the next three years, a mournful period that left her feeling overwhelmed. In January 1964, her old professor Mae Neptune also passed away. Dovey's grandmother Rachel, who had done more to nurture her and shape her than anyone else, took her last breath later that year. Like Professor Neptune, she died at ninety years old. Rachel had been Dovey's rock against the wind, her shelter whenever the storms of fortune struck her and shook her to her core. No matter what had happened to upset Dovey, she had been able to turn to her grandmother for comfort and timely advice. In low moments, such as the breakup of her marriage, and in moments of triumph, such as her victory in the *Keys* case, Dovey had always returned to Rachel's home and found her waiting with open arms, a delicious meal simmering on the stove behind her. At fifty years old, Dovey had more than grief to contend with. She was battling her own infirmities, including diabetes.

Meanwhile, the United States was immersed in its own trials and tribulations. Medgar Evers, a brilliant civil rights leader, had been assassinated in Jackson, Mississippi, on June 12, 1963. His death came little more than a month after public safety commissioner Eugene "Bull" Connor had turned fire hoses on children and other protesters during a demonstration in Birmingham, Alabama. In September of that year, less than a month after Rev. Martin Luther King Jr. shared his dream at the March on Washington, terrorists planted a bomb in Birmingham's Sixteenth Street Baptist Church.

Four little Black girls died in the explosion. In November, the entire country mourned when President John F. Kennedy was fatally shot in Dallas. Sorrow turned into resolve during the summer of 1964, when student activists journeyed down South to register Black citizens to vote. In June three of them—James Chaney, Mickey Schwerner, and Andrew Goodman—were found murdered in Philadelphia, Mississippi. The killings stunned and repulsed many Americans and brought more attention to the expanding struggle for civil rights. On one hand, the events attracted supporters

Mourners exit Sixteenth Street Baptist Church in Birmingham, Alabama, after the funeral for the four girls killed in the bombing of the church on September 15, 1963.

for African American activists, but on the other, they exposed the country's divisions. The United States was heading toward a fateful reckoning. Either it would finally honor the rights and liberties proclaimed in its Constitution, or it would risk everything by refusing to do so.

Like many other Americans dealing with such loss and turmoil, Dovey poured her feelings into prayer in hopes of easing her aching soul. She remembered Rev. King's words at the March on Washington, when he'd urged his audience to hold out hope for "the high road of peace" that would eventually come.

Dovey:

I wanted to believe that, and my religious faith demanded that I do so. But I struggled mightily to square my fundamental belief in human goodness with the brutality that came in waves, each more hideous than the last, as though the country was caught in some kind of monstrous and protracted birthing process that gave way at last to the signing of the Civil Rights Act of 1964.

She also devoted countless hours to serving the needs of parishioners at her church, Allen Chapel. In 1961, just three and a half weeks after Julius died, she had been ordained an itinerant deacon in the AME Church. Two years after that she'd become an itinerant elder. Her new status enabled her to perform all the duties of an AME minister, including preaching, presiding at weddings and funerals, and baptizing the faithful.

By 1964, Dovey was also busy with expanding her legal practice. After purchasing a rowhouse a few doors down from the office she had shared with Julius, she hired architects and builders to transform it from a mortuary into a full-service law office. She rented part of the space to attorneys George Knox and Bruce Harrison, who were her friends as well as her colleagues. Jerry Hunter, Dovey's cousin and

Rev. Dovey Johnson Roundtree with Rev. James A. Williamson on the steps of Washington's Allen Chapel AME Church, where she served as an associate pastor.

a student at Howard Law School, was also often on hand. While these men were more than capable, none of them could replace Julius.

Dovey:

> *I'd been reared to keep up a good front in public, to behave as though I was fearless even when I didn't feel that way, and I daresay not even those close to me saw how deeply I grieved. I missed Julius more than I'd thought possible, missed his brilliance and his common sense and his hardheadedness and his*

"what difference does it make if you're a woman"
attitude. I also missed his protective presence,
though I wouldn't have admitted that to a living
soul.

Some of the clients Dovey met in her new office were genuine troublemakers. They created difficulties for themselves by inflicting violence or harm on other people. Some clients, though, found themselves in trouble that they hadn't done anything to attract; the only thing they had done was end up in the wrong place at the wrong time. Of the latter group, she had seldom encountered anyone as troubled as Raymond Crump. Even so, he was more than just another troubled client.

In late October 1964, Dovey walked through the doors of the DC jail and saw Crump for the first time. Short in stature and slightly built, he sat fidgeting in a chair, his eyes darting around the room. "Lawyer," he said to Dovey, "what is it they say I done?"

His question came on the heels of a grisly discovery. On October 12, the body of a forty-three-year-old woman had been found near the Chesapeake and Ohio Canal in the section of Washington, DC, known as Georgetown. Shot twice at close range while struggling with her attacker, Mary Pinchot Meyer had been white, affluent, and popular. Her death had been covered in the local papers. And a prominent article in the *New York Times* made it clear that Meyer's death was a national story. WOMAN PAINTER SHOT AND KILLED ON CANAL TOWPATH IN CAPITAL, the headline read. All the articles described her as a friend of Mrs. Jacqueline Kennedy, the former First Lady.

It would be years before Dovey learned that there was much more to the story than the newspaper accounts revealed. Washington gossip circulating at the time of the trial hinted vaguely that Meyer's closeness with the Kennedys might have given her access to secrets that influential people didn't want revealed. But the fact that Mary Meyer had kept a diary that included sensitive details about President Kennedy remained hidden until a decade after the murder. Eventually, all of Washington would learn that on the night of her murder, her brother-in-law, prominent newspaperman Ben Bradlee, along with a high official in the Central Intelligence Agency (CIA), had broken into

Washington socialite and White House insider Mary Pinchot Meyer, pictured here at President John F. Kennedy's forty-sixth birthday party.

her apartment, discovered the diary, and hidden it. Bradlee revealed this in his memoir, published thirty years after the fact. At the time, Dovey knew only that the movers and shakers in Washington were using all their power to ensure that the case was quickly solved and forgotten. Until then, the mystery of Meyer's murder would have the city's full attention.

The killing had been committed in broad daylight, not far from busy streets crowded with potential witnesses. To carry out the crime, authorities had concluded, the killer must have been quick, bold, and clever. They insisted that the killer had to have been Raymond Crump. He claimed that he'd been found near the crime scene because he had been fishing close by. Police had dismissed his alibi and charged him with first-degree murder. If convicted, he would almost certainly have been executed for the crime.

Crump, however, was neither quick nor bold nor clever. He drank too much and had been in minor scrapes, but he had no record of violent behavior. Undersized and slow to react, he had been bullied throughout much of his youth. Although he was twenty-four years old, married, and the father of five children, Crump acted as if he were several years younger. His mother, Martha Crump, believed fiercely in her son's innocence. When she'd brought his case to Dovey, Mrs. Crump had said that she regarded her son as a child in a man's body. Observing Crump during their first jailhouse interview, Dovey was inclined to agree. Her new client seemed hardly able to hold a conversation; his ability to plan a murder and carry it out seemed highly unlikely.

Dovey:

> *When I met with Raymond Crump for the first time in the DC jail, the word that came to my mind was "incapable." He was, I remember thinking, incapable of clear communication, incapable of complex thought, incapable of grasping the full weight of his predicament, incapable, most of all, of a murder executed with the stealth and precision and forethought of Mary Meyer's . . . That the little slip of a man sitting before me in a state of such bewilderment could have planned, perpetrated, and hidden a crime of that magnitude struck me as preposterous.*

Leaning across the table, she put her two hands on both of his and slowly explained the charge he faced.

Trembling in his seat, Crump denied any wrongdoing. He also told Dovey that the policeman who'd arrested him had tried to beat a confession out of him. The cop had responded to Crump's denials by beating him even harder. Dovey was aware of jailhouse beatings, but she had thought—hoped— they were a thing of the past. She reconsidered, however, watching in horror as Crump began to cry. "I didn't shoot nobody," he said.

Dovey placed her business card in his hand. Then she fixed her gaze on him until he was compelled to look directly into her eyes. "I'm here to look out for you, Raymond," she told him. "If anyone bothers you, I want to know about it right away. If you're frightened, and I'm not here, call out my name as loud as you can. Tell 'em, 'My lawyer's on her way.'"

CHAPTER 9

DEFENDING RAYMOND CRUMP

In the case of *United States v. Raymond Crump Jr.*, the federal government had a full array of resources at its command, including an aggressive prosecutor with a generous budget, plus a team of assistants supported by highly skilled investigators and the Washington, DC, police department. On her side, Dovey had George Knox, formerly her tenant and now her partner; law student Jerry Hunter; and a single assistant, Purcell Moore, who functioned as a private detective for her. In terms of money, influence, news coverage, and personnel, she was outnumbered and outgunned. To make matters worse, Crump had lied about fishing in the Potomac River; he had actually been with a woman that morning. Had Crump been truthful, the lack of physical evidence might well have been sufficient to raise reasonable doubt. But he had lied. And that had created a real problem for Dovey. Still, she believed she could save Crump's life if she fought hard enough.

The DC police department wasted no time using the tools at their disposal. To find the .38-caliber Smith & Wesson pistol that had killed Mary Meyer, law enforcement officials launched a search so extensive and costly that it caused Dovey to wonder whether there was more to this case than met the eye. Why was the government going to such extremes to ensure a conviction? In the forty-eight hours after the murder, teams of police officers, walking four and five abreast, scoured the crime scene, including the woods bordering the canal. When their efforts proved futile, a team of navy divers was employed to examine the canal and the Potomac River. That search, too, was fruitless, so the FBI drained the canal, sifted the mud at the bottom, and used minesweepers to scan the canal bed.

Not only did they fail to find a gun connected to Crump, but they found no gun at all. There was no evidence that he had ever owned a weapon, and, Dovey discovered, there was no evidence linking him to the victim. There were no powder burns on his fingers to show that he'd recently discharged a firearm. And while there was blood at the crime scene, there was no blood on Crump.

Scuba divers search for a weapon on the Chesapeake and Ohio Canal near where Mary Meyer was murdered. No weapon was ever found.

Police had arrested him solely on the basis of statements from three men who'd claimed to be witnesses. The first, a military man jogging on his lunch hour, Lieutenant William L. Mitchell, had come to police the day after the murder claiming that while he'd been running on the canal towpath, he had passed within three feet of a Black man who appeared to be trailing Mary Meyer. The other two were auto mechanics who'd said they'd heard gunshots and screams while working on a stalled car on a nearby thoroughfare. One of them claimed he'd seen a Black man standing over the body before placing something in his pocket and walking toward the woods.

At a coroner's inquest held before Dovey took the case, none of these alleged witnesses had actually testified. The only testimony came from the DC police detective in charge of the case. He spoke on behalf of the witnesses, sharing accounts he said they'd given him. Courts often dismiss such testimony as hearsay, but in Crump's case the court moved forward. By the time Dovey began representing the defendant, the court had decided that a preliminary hearing would be unnecessary. She would have no opportunity to compel the witnesses to appear in court by means of a subpoena, cross-examine them, or learn how the government was constructing its case. Dovey filed a writ of habeas corpus, which is a demand that the government either produce sufficient evidence for holding a person accused of a crime or release him. But the court declined to take it seriously. She was left without the trail of documents that attorneys rely on when preparing their defense. So she decided to focus her initial efforts on the *actual* trail, the path the murderer would have taken while committing his crime and leaving the scene.

With her associates George and Jerry, she walked the length of the canal, exploring the surrounding woods, the towpath, and the stone wall where the mechanic claimed he'd stood and seen the killer. As she worked, Dovey formed a picture in her mind of every single detail. Soon the trees, stones, and surrounding vegetation became as recognizable to her as the furniture in her own home. She also visualized the crime as it had happened, the horrible possibilities. A woman walking alone, relaxing in familiar surroundings, a man lurking in the shadows with malice on his mind. Day after day throughout November and December, Dovey and her colleagues repeated every possible scenario, trying to track the killer's movements, tracing the alleged witnesses' lines of sight, imagining the gunshots and the screams. They even smashed paper bags to mimic the sound of a weapon firing.

Her investigation convinced her that none of the witnesses had actually seen Meyer's killer leave the scene. In mid-October thick foliage had covered the trees—and obscured the murderer as he made his getaway. Dovey noted other weaknesses in the government's failure to find a weapon, the absence of any physical evidence, and the questionable statements made by the alleged witnesses. She faced steep odds, it was true, but when she considered these flaws together, she began to see a slender possibility of victory.

If Dovey had known about Mary Meyer's possible access to government secrets, she might not have been puzzled by certain curious incidents. During her examinations of the crime scene, she often had the feeling that she was being watched, that there was, as she would recall years later, "something sinister" about it all. Soon she began to receive mysterious phone calls.

Dovey:

I cannot pinpoint the date on which I received the first phone call in the middle of the night that shattered the peace of my household and left me with the sense that my investigations along the canal had not gone unnoticed. But I remember the queasy feeling with great clarity, for I knew then, and felt more and more definitely as the weeks passed and the calls continued, that my movements were being tracked by someone with a keen interest in the outcome of the trial. Sometime after midnight the phone would ring. The caller never spoke, yet he or she stayed on the line, breathing into the phone until I hung up. Days would pass, and then once again would come the dreaded ring. The calls, it became clear, were tied to my visits to the crime scene. The more we visited the crime scene, the more persistent the calls became.

Inside the DC jail, Crump's condition seemed to be declining. He was fearful of the white prison guards, whose hatred for him Dovey had seen with her own eyes. She was sure they believed that Crump was guilty and deserved the death penalty. As weeks turned into months, he began to show signs of the constant pressure placed on him to confess to the killing. Reluctant to leave his cell, he began to eat less because he thought his food was being poisoned. His wife had abandoned him and fled the city, leaving his mother as the only family member who supported him. Crump grew more suspicious of nearly everyone except Dovey. She decided to show up at the jail every day, both to reassure her client and discourage others from thinking about harming him.

While protecting Crump as best as she could, Dovey continued to develop her case. The prosecution stymied her efforts, refusing to provide even its list of witnesses and exhibits. With the paper trail growing alarmingly thin, Dovey pored over the police files in hopes of finding some stray detail that could strengthen her defense. She found it in a document from the coroner's inquest. The police detective, reporting what the auto mechanic had seen, had said he'd described the man standing over the corpse as five feet eight inches tall and weighing 185 pounds. The jogger's description of the man he'd passed put him at five feet eight, though he did not provide a weight estimate. Whoever the man was, he wasn't Raymond Crump. Dovey's client stood five feet three inches tall and weighed 130 pounds.

Dovey pondered how best to use this discovery as the summer of 1965 began to unfold. African Americans were

An Alabama state trooper clubs John Lewis, leader of the Student
Nonviolent Coordinating Committee (SNCC), during an attempted march
from Selma to Montgomery on March 7, 1965.

still recovering from the March 7 clash between police and
civil rights protesters on the Edmund Pettus Bridge outside
Selma, Alabama. The police had set upon the unarmed civil-
ians with whips, clubs, and tear gas, in an incident that would
be remembered as Bloody Sunday. The conflict, the latest in
a series of violent episodes, had discouraged activists and
their supporters across the country. Black people had begun
to wonder whether they could get a fair chance at justice
anywhere.

The question hung in the air on July 20, when Raymond Crump finally got his day in court.

Dovey:

> *My very presence, I knew, irritated and threatened many of the white judges and lawyers in the court-house, male and female alike. There'd been bitter pro-tests just a year or so earlier when my name had been proposed for membership in the all-white DC Wom-en's Bar Association by the brave and bold attor-ney Joyce Hens Green. There were board members who'd resigned over the matter, and it had required all of Joyce Green's influence to force the issue to a vote of the entire membership, something that had never been done before. I sat in the US District Court on the first morning of the Crump trial keenly aware that there were many who wanted me to fail.*

Over eight days, the government introduced more than twenty witnesses, including every policeman who had been at the scene, the jogger, the mechanics, a government map-maker, and several crime experts. The prosecutor, US Attor-ney Alfred Hantman, had also mounted more than fifty exhibits, including a fifty-five-foot map of the crime scene and a bloodstained tree trunk. The victim had clung to it, he claimed, during the last minutes of her life.

The fourth-floor courtroom in the US District Court for the District of Columbia was packed every day, crammed with reporters, members of Martha Crump's church, and a few well-dressed friends of Mary Pinchot Meyer. They listened carefully as the government laid out its case, and so did Dovey. She planned to tread lightly, watch, and make her move when she saw an opening.

Her first opening came on the second day of trial, when US Attorney Hantman called the government's mapmaker to the stand to testify about the possible exits to the crime scene. As the jury looked at the giant map of the scene mounted on the courtroom wall, the mapmaker testified that the crime scene had only four possible escape routes. During her cross-examination, Dovey gently pressed the witness until he admitted that there were in fact many ways for a man to leave the park if he stepped off the paths and entered the woods. Dovey's multiple trips to the crime scene and her painstaking reenactments had begun to pay off. She had become quite familiar with the towpath, the canal, and the surrounding roads. In contrast, the expert had never set foot in the area.

When the most important government witness of all took the stand, Dovey was ready for him. Mechanic Henry Wiggins claimed to have seen a Black man standing over the body of Mary Meyer. Dovey pressed him to repeat his description of the suspect as five feet eight inches and 185 pounds. He wilted under Dovey's fierce grilling, finally conceding that he couldn't be sure Crump was the man he'd seen. "I didn't look at him that hard," he confessed. The courtroom went still. Dovey looked at the jury, at each of their shocked faces. And then she turned back to Wiggins. "Did you ever, Mr. Witness, look at this man hard?" Wiggins did not reply.

But the jurors continued to study Raymond as the trial moved into its third day. As one police officer after another took the stand to recount the height description given on the police lookout based on Wiggins's information, the jury followed Raymond as he walked in each day, stood beside Dovey, took his seat at the defense table. When the jogger took the stand, he was unable to identify Crump as the man he'd seen. He said only that the man he'd passed was five feet eight. After planting that height estimate firmly in the jurors' minds, Dovey went on to remind them that the prosecution had not a shred of physical evidence, including the gun or bloodstains, to link her client to the crime. Raymond Crump had been brought to the bar of justice on the word of a single witness who now admitted he'd hardly glanced at the suspected killer. As the trial neared its end, Dovey retreated each evening to her screened porch to ponder what had begun as a little case for a little man.

Dovey:

I thought much of Raymond each evening as I rocked on my porch swing and scribbled on my

legal pad, of the human being I'd struggled to pro-
tect from the destructive forces of prison, the human
being in whose innocence I believed, and whose life
I was trying to save. Raymond Crump was not a
great man, to be sure. He had none of the qualities
of mind that the world prizes. He was limited in his
mental powers . . . He was the sort of person society
considered so expendable that if he were subtracted
from the human population, no one would miss him
except his mother. But he was a human being, and
he counted in the eye of the Lord, and the eye of
the law as well, which regards men as God does, all
equal one to another.

Dovey's case was twenty minutes long and consisted of three witnesses from Raymond's church, who testified to his good character as a man of peace and good order. When these witnesses had finished, Dovey rested her case.

The prosecutor was stunned. "Your Honor," he said, "I am caught completely flat-footed at this time. I never in my wildest dreams anticipated that counsel would rest her case."

But Dovey had done all that she needed to do. The prosecution had handed her her case, and she'd tried it.

When she rose to deliver her closing argument, she walked to the jury box and looked each person in the eye. She felt as if everything she'd done over the course of her lifetime had been moving her toward this moment. She thought of Grandma Rachel, of Miss Neptune, Dr. Bethune, and Professor Nabrit. Every principle for which they'd taught her to fight—equality, dignity, and the right to live freely in peace—was on trial alongside Raymond Crump.

"I told you in my opening," she began, "that one exhibit you had before you for eight days. You had it from the moment you took this case—Raymond Crump Jr. When you go into the jury room, you will take with you his image, and you must answer, I submit, the question: Does he weigh one hundred eighty-five pounds? That was the lookout given to the world at large, that there was a man five feet eight on the towpath that did indeed murder this poor lady. This is not Raymond Crump Jr."

The case that had seemed so complicated, she told the jurors, was actually quite simple.

The height and weight discrepancy alone, she said, was enough to create reasonable doubt in anyone's mind. But there was more. Or rather, less. The prosecution had produced no weapon. No fiber linking Raymond to the victim, or her to him. No fingerprints. No powder burns. No blood on Raymond's clothing.

"I say to you, you must have reasonable doubt from all of the evidence that has been adduced before you," she said. "You must have reasonable doubt, if for no other reason than that the dimensions of the person out on the towpath, the dimensions of the person seen by two persons, exact in every particular, simply do not fit Raymond Crump Jr."

She looked into the faces of the jury as she drove home her final point about Raymond himself.

"We have brought you character witnesses who testified before you this morning. Perhaps when I called them, you said: Well, she is not giving much evidence. I gave you the most important evidence anyone can present for another person."

Dovey paused, and quoted a line from Shakespeare's *Othello*, the play she had learned to love so many years ago in Miss Neptune's classroom at Spelman:

"He who steals from me my purse steals trash, but take away from me my—what?—my good name, and you have taken all that I have."

She turned and looked at Raymond and then back at the jury.

"I leave this little man in your hands."

Silence descended on the courtroom as the members of the jury returned.

"Mr. Foreman," the clerk asked, "has the jury agreed upon a verdict?"

"It has."

The clerk handed the slip of paper to Judge Corcoran and asked the defendant to rise.

"Members of the jury," said the judge, "we have your verdict, which states that you find the defendant Ray Crump Jr. not guilty. And this is your verdict, so say you each and all?"

The jurors nodded.

"Raymond Crump," Judge Corcoran said, "you are a free man."

After ten months in jail, after endless hours under the watch of hateful guards, Raymond Crump could go where he pleased. His freedom proved the wisdom of Justice John Marshall Harlan's dissent in *Plessy*, the words that had so moved Dovey during her law school days. "There is no caste here," the justice had written. "Our Constitution is color-blind, and neither knows nor tolerates classes among its citizens. In respect of civil rights, all citizens are equal before the law. The humblest is the peer of the most powerful. The law regards man as man, and takes no account of his surroundings or of his color when his civil rights as guaranteed by the supreme law of the land are involved."

In Grandma Rachel's time, the southern states barred Black people from serving on juries or testifying during a trial. A generation later, it was still often unthinkable for an African American to appear in court as anything other than a defendant. During most of the country's existence, for a Black person to be acquitted of a sensational crime involving a white victim was almost unimaginable. Dovey had turned nearly two hundred years of criminal-justice history upside down. And, as she would say years later, her victory "made it impossible for the matter of Mary Pinchot Meyer's murder to be sealed off and forgotten, as the government so clearly wanted to do." The case remains unsolved to this day, but researchers have continued to probe what Dovey called "the troubling circumstances" surrounding Meyer's murder.

If Raymond was thinking of such matters, he gave no sign. All he wanted, he told Dovey, was to go home.

As flashbulbs popped and reporters rushed to file their stories, Martha Crump rejoiced at her son's great fortune. Beside her, Raymond basked in the freedom he had sorely missed. Dovey, packing her papers into the briefcase Mae Neptune had given her years before, paused to reflect on her unlikely victory. More than any other case, *United States v. Raymond Crump Jr.* had defined her very essence as a lawyer. And it led her, ultimately, to move beyond the law.

CHAPTER 10

JUSTICE OLDER THAN THE LAW

Dovey's triumph in the *Keys* case was part of a celebrated wave of advances in civil rights law. In contrast, her victory in the *Crump* case brought a different kind of acclaim. Until her defeat of an aggressive, well-funded prosecutor and his powerful political allies, criminal trials had seldom been seen as places where Black lawyers could obtain a fair hearing, to say nothing of an acquittal. In the months and years that followed, her newfound notoriety brought more opportunities than most lawyers dreamed possible. Judges assigned her to complicated murder cases that other attorneys found too intimidating to take on. Again and again, Dovey won acquittals for defendants who faced nearly insurmountable odds.

As with her earlier courtroom successes, the outcome created more opportunities for the generation of Black lawyers who came after her. Remembering Mae Neptune's urgent insistence that she "pass it on," she convened informal legal seminars in her office. The sessions enabled her to share her experience and insights with younger colleagues, coaching them on the finer points of the law, much as mentors like Professor James Madison Nabrit had done for her. Dovey proudly realized that her conquest in the district courthouse had made it easier for women attorneys—as well as attorneys from other ethnic or racial backgrounds—to walk those same halls.

Even in the midst of her joy, Dovey couldn't help noticing reasons for concern. She became more and more aware of a creeping sense of hopelessness, moving like a cloud of noxious fumes through the streets and alleys of the Black neighborhoods she'd come to love. This formless despair went beyond her adopted city of Washington and penetrated African American communities across the country. Every time her people made an advance, some new setback seemed to emerge and challenge their progress.

In the summer of 1965, about a week after she won Raymond Crump's acquittal, Congress passed the Voting Rights Act. The new legislation, which included sweeping reforms meant to grant all Americans equal access to ballot boxes and polling booths, was cause for wary celebration. But its passage

Riots broke out in cities across America in the wake of the assassination of
the Reverend Martin Luther King Jr. on April 4, 1968.

was followed almost immediately by the Watts rebellion. In that Los Angeles neighborhood, Black residents had protested police brutality by fighting policemen, blocking traffic, and destroying businesses. Thirty-four people died, more than a thousand were injured, and thousands more were arrested. Similar uprisings took place in other cities over the next few years. African Americans, realizing it had required more than half a century to bring down Jim Crow, feared that removing its effects would take just as long. Frustrated, many took to the streets with increasing fury. Their anger peaked in 1968, after the assassination of Rev. Martin Luther King

Jr. Dovey watched as Black Washington went up in flames. As smoke billowed from buildings not far from her office on Eleventh Street, sirens screamed, and people rushed frantically past her.

In the years that followed, rage often gave way to despair as cities crumbled under modern pressures. Inner-city areas remained in ruins, slow to recover from the damage the riots had inflicted. New interstate highways disrupted some Black communities and completely displaced others. Police brutality, a nationwide shortage of jobs, and rising costs of living all contributed to an epidemic of drug abuse. Crime and violence spread like contagious diseases, poisoning families, schools, entire neighborhoods. In Dovey's view, these troubling changes inflicted the most harm on the individuals least able to defend themselves: children.

Dovey:

> More and more, as I labored at the bar and in the pulpit and in the privacy of the counseling room, I confronted shattered children, children caught between warring parents, children who'd borne witness to the most horrific crimes, children neglected and shunted aside, children preyed upon by those entrusted with their care. Seeing this, I began to shift the direction of my law practice in the seventies and

eighties, even as I had chosen a different path in the fifties, in the wake of the Sarah Keys *case. I threw myself into another war, a war for the children.*

Rev. Dovey Roundtree mingles with her congregation after
services at Allen Chapel AME Church, circa 1990.

As one decade rolled into another, Dovey's law practice intersected more and more with her ministry at Allen Chapel. The two callings became so connected that an observer would have had difficulty telling one from the other. Her mission on behalf of children became even more personal in 1992, when she was seventy-eight. That year, her family expanded in a wonderful and unexpected way.

Dovey:

In the magnificent young woman named Charlene Pritchett, who came into my life on a Sunday morning when she gave me a ride home from services at Allen Chapel, I found not only a companion and helpmate in my increasing infirmity, but a true and faithful and much beloved daughter. And in her son, James Andrew, I was given a grandson, and a whole world.

Dovey Johnson Roundtree, circa 1985, on the steps of US District Court for the District of Columbia.

Dovey practiced law until she was in her eighties, before moving with Charlene and James Andrew to a life of retirement in Spotsylvania, Virginia, and from there to her childhood home in Charlotte. Until then, she represented youthful defendants in juvenile court, protecting them as much as she could from the damaging influence of gang violence, jails, and prisons. At the same time, she spent long hours trying custody cases in family court, working hard to secure peace between angry spouses. Whether she was representing the mother or the father, she fought for the children they shared. Dovey's appearances before judges and court officials, her negotiations with angry parents, and her interviews with their suffering children convinced her that the law could not solve so many new and challenging problems all by itself.

Nor could the church, she realized, but she was determined to use both of her missions to serve the same goal. Far too often she was called upon to preside over services in which young victims of gang violence were laid to rest. Remembrances of the young people slain often mixed with defiant calls for vengeance. Dovey's task involved calming the fierce emotions of the bereaved while helping them to accept a reality that no one could claim to make sense of: the murder of a child by other children. Risking the anger of the assembled mourners, she would call for compassion for both the family of the dead and the child who'd pulled the trigger.

Dovey Roundtree, circa 1980, speaking at an AME Church conference in Memphis, Tennessee.

"He's out there somewhere," she'd tell them. "He, too, needs our love."

She took this message beyond the pulpit of Allen Chapel to the podiums at legal conventions, conferences, and professional gatherings around the nation. Wherever she addressed an audience, she urged her listeners to take youngsters' needs seriously. As long as she was able, she spoke passionately on their behalf. Throughout her career, she had battled for equality and fairness—in the army, in her exhausting campaign against Jim Crow, in hundreds of court cases. None of those important endeavors, she realized, was as pressing as the fight for the future of African American children. The kind of justice she envisioned was older than the law itself and resided in people's hearts.

She argued that no one could play the part of an innocent bystander while the forces of violence, monstrous and hungry, devoured society's youngest members. She believed that no children were beyond redemption, especially if they were ministered to in the same way that her grandmother had ministered to her.

In her final years, Dovey battled for justice not in the church or courtroom, but rather on long walks with James, where she shared her "Grandma stories," as James called them. She'd tell him of how Grandma Rachel would stand out on the front porch and shake her fist at the lightning, of how on summer mornings, when everyone else was still asleep, she'd take Dovey into the forest just before sunrise to pick blackberries, call to the birds, and watch the sun come up.

Dovey:

> One story cannot change the world, I know. But one child can. In every child like my James Andrew, there is infinite potential, untarnished and whole, and it is in ministering to our children that we stand to alter the future. It took James to teach me the final lesson about King's "beloved community," and to make me believe,

really believe, that it could be achieved. It took James,
too, to bring me to a full understanding of the miracle
making of my grandmother, of what she accomplished
in the humblest ministrations of daily life.

It was the responsibility of every adult, she argued, not just parents and pastors and teachers, to raise children up in love and kindness, to shower them with affection and guide them with example and instruction. To wrap them in a warm embrace from the moment they were born. To say to them, you are never alone, although sometimes you might feel like it. You belong to all of us. You are our children. You are as good as anybody.

Dovey's approach to the practice of law and the act of ministry had been shaped by wise and loving teachers. From each of them—

Dovey Roundtree with her goddaughter's son, James Andrew Pritchett, after a 2001 Women's History Month event at the US Government Printing Office, where she delivered a speech on the crisis of urban violence.

Edythe Wimbish, Mae Neptune, Dr. Bethune, and Professor Nabrit—she had acquired some key lesson or skill she needed to succeed. Still, it was the wisdom of Grandma Rachel that she turned to most often, all the days of her life.

Dovey:

> *With all the ugliness outside us in Charlotte, it was good around our table. It was good when Mama sang, and Grandma hummed. It was good when Grandpa brought home a watermelon, or a cantaloupe, or a bushel of ripe tomatoes for Grandma to can, or a sack of peaches we'd peel for pies, and, every once in a while, steal a slice on the sly. That was good. That was good good. All of that hurt, out there and over there, somehow could not and did not disturb that sense of precious fellowship that Grandma created with corn pudding, or rice pudding, or bread pudding with raisins all plumped up. She is the reason I am able to look at the darkness and confusion of our times, and know that if we minister to our children as she ministered to me, redemption is truly possible. It is, indeed, inevitable.*

AUTHOR'S NOTE

"I have found that there is always somebody who would be the miracle-maker in your life, if you but believe."

The words were so utterly improbable, coming as they did from a lawyer, that they brought me up short in my reading of the *Washington Post* on a February morning in 1995, and I looked, hard, at the photograph of the elderly African American woman who had spoken them. She had the most penetrating eyes, eyes that seemed to look directly at me. This, I remember thinking, was a human being who'd known great pain as well as great joy, who exuded warmth but brooked no foolishness. Her name, according to the article accompanying the photograph, was Dovey Johnson Roundtree, and she had inspired actress Cicely Tyson in her portrayal of a maverick civil rights lawyer in the television series *Sweet Justice*. Who was she, this lawyer who'd practiced law for forty years in the city where I'd grown up, who'd made civil rights history, who'd taken on cases other lawyers ran from, and won them?

And this, in an all-white judicial system? Why had I never heard of her?

On that day twenty-six years ago, I set out on the journey that led to publication of the book that became *Mighty Justice*. At the outset, I wanted simply to write a profile of Dovey Roundtree for *Washingtonian* magazine. What I did not know then, what I could never have imagined on that cold winter morning when she first ushered me into her tiny law office for the interview I'd requested, was the extent to which Dovey—this lawyer who spoke so eloquently of miracles—would become the miracle-maker in my own life.

From the time we met until her death in 2018, Dovey gave me the gifts of her time, her wisdom, her friendship, her support of me and my family, and the breathtaking example of her unflagging faith. And in a world riven by racial hurt and anger, she gave me her trust. She was a Black woman born in the early twentieth century in the Jim Crow South. I am a white woman who came of age in 1950s Washington, DC. And yet Dovey chose to enter into a critical partnership with me, to bring me into her home, enfold me into her family, and share with me over more than a decade not only the facts of her life but also her doubts, her sorrow, and the pain of race and gender exclusion she called "a rusty nail upon my heart."

I put endless questions to her in my search for understanding. And Dovey rose up with the entirety of her being with responses that often took my breath away. She filled the room with the force of her vision. She spoke with a depth and honesty that told me she believed I could in fact understand her worldview and her suffering, despite all the apparent differences between us.

This, of course, did not happen all at once. As I raced after her to court, to her home at the edge of Rock Creek Park, to the Anacostia church where she ministered, she was watching me as closely as I was watching her. I could barely keep up with her, despite the fact that she was an eighty-two-year-old diabetic with arthritis and failing eyesight who navigated the courtrooms and streets with a walker, and I was half her age and in perfect health.

Drawn to her fierce passion for justice and her mesmerizing eloquence, I followed wherever she led, and along the way I became convinced that the magazine article I'd set out to write about her life could not possibly encompass even the bare facts of it, let alone its animating spirit. In the half century of her career, she'd walked with nearly every giant of the American civil rights movement, breaking barriers herself at every turn. And she had a vision of justice so vital and transformative it needed a book to contain it.

I'll never forget the day I told her that, nor the clarity of her response.

"I believe there's a book in your life, Mrs. Roundtree," I said, not yet quite ready to address her, as I eventually came to do, as Dovey, or Dove.

"Why?" she asked, her brow furrowing. This, I remember thinking, must be what it felt like to be deposed by her prior to a trial. I said that her life had great historical significance and that the world needed to hear about it directly from her. I explained that I couldn't devote my full time to the book until I cleared my other writing obligations and that this was an undertaking that would almost certainly require years. Dovey closed her eyes and shook her head.

"I don't have time," she said. "I'm eighty-three years old. I need to hurry."

So I threw myself into the listener role, and Dovey talked, and talked, and talked, and we embarked on a book together. We formed a bond that survived her move from Washington to her Charlotte, North Carolina, home as she became increasingly incapacitated by her diabetes. That bond survived her blindness, my slowness, and our fear that we might not complete our work in time. She and I could never have anticipated, as we threw in our lots together to write a book on speculation, what our collaboration would produce.

Since the time of Dovey's death in 2018, at the age of 104, her story has generated feature-film interest and made possible the creation of scholarships in her name for deserving Spelman College and Howard Law School students. It has also inspired a picture book for young children as well as this middle-grade edition, adapted from the original work in a way that transcends mere summary to fully honor Dovey's voice. This young readers' edition preserves not only the structure of our book but also Dovey's own words, interweaving passages from *Mighty Justice* into every chapter of the narrative so that children can experience the force and beauty of Dovey's spirit.

I am sorry that Dovey did not live to see this book, because she believed so deeply in our obligation to young people. From every pulpit to which she was given access in the final years of her life, she spoke of the need to sustain and nurture the next generation. For Dovey, children were far more than an abstract cause. Though she had no children of her own, she had James Andrew Pritchett, the son of her beloved goddaughter Charlene Pritchett-Stevenson—for whom she cared with the intensity of a grandparent. She looked at every child who crossed her path in terms of their potential, and in the twenty-four years I knew Dovey, I never once saw her pass up a child. That is how I know she would have loved this book.

"Pass it on," her beloved Spelman mentor Mae Neptune told Dovey in 1937, when the professor arranged the loan that enabled Dovey to finish college. Now, more than eighty years later, with the release of this book for young readers, the passing on continues.

Dovey Roundtree and coauthor Katie McCabe at the 2006 Thurgood Marshall Awards dinner in Charlotte, North Carolina, where Dovey was honored.

DISCUSSION QUESTIONS

1. *Mighty Justice* begins with two stories of injustice, one suffered by Dovey's grandmother as a girl, the other by the young Dovey herself. It ends with a grand vision of justice. What are the turning points in Dovey's journey from experiencing an unjust world to envisioning a just one?

2. How was Dovey affected both as a child and over the course of her lifetime by the story of Grandma Rachel's broken feet and by participating in her grandmother's nightly foot-washing ritual? What larger significance do you find in this story? How was Grandma Rachel a life-long model of courage for Dovey?

3. During Dovey's Spelman College years, she had crucial experiences with two white women who were opposites in terms of their racial attitudes—one punished Dovey's educational goals by accusing her of stealing and

having her arrested, and the other mentored her and loaned her money to finish college. In what ways was Dovey changed by these contrasting interactions?

4. How was Dovey influenced at Spelman by Black intellectuals such as W. E. B. Du Bois?

5. Dovey writes of her time in the army, "I entered the military a girl doing the bidding of others, living out the dream of a great leader, and marching to her orders. I left it a woman grown." How did Dovey find her voice in the military?

6. Dovey was extremely proud of her military service. How did she eventually move past her anger at Jim Crow in the military and in the country? Do you consider yourself patriotic, and what do you think it means to be patriotic?

7. How did Dovey experience sexism during law school? What communities and individuals helped her survive this form of prejudice? How was her classmate and eventual law partner, Julius Robertson, different from the other men she met in law school?

8. Dovey referred to the 1896 US Supreme Court case

Plessy v. Ferguson as a lie. What did she mean by that? How would you describe the larger consequences of Dovey's limited win in her Jim Crow lawsuit on behalf of her mother and grandmother against Southern Railway?

9. What elements of *Sarah Keys v. Carolina Coach Company* give it a similar historical significance to that of the Rosa Parks case? How was it groundbreaking?

10. During the six-year period between the Interstate Commerce Commission's *Keys* ruling in 1955 and the time when it finally took effect in 1961, Dovey writes, she "became a different person, a different sort of lawyer, in fact, from the one who'd battled the ICC. I am not sure that I chose that path, so much as it chose me." What does she mean?

11. What part did Grandma Rachel and other people play in Dovey's decision to study for the ministry in a church that did not at that time permit the ordination of women? What other factors influenced her to go in that direction?

12. Over the course of Dovey's life, she had many mentors, mostly Black but some white. What role did each of

these people play in Dovey's formation? What do you think makes for a good mentor?

13. In what ways is Dovey a role model for the next generation in the fight for social justice?

IMPORTANT CIVIL RIGHTS COURT CASES

Dovey Roundtree's groundbreaking bus desegregation case, *Keys v. Carolina Coach Company*, was one milestone in a long, complicated series of legal victories that shattered "separate but equal." To help readers better understand how the *Keys* case fits into the journey out of Jim Crow, the following list of cases is provided, with short summaries of each one.

TRANSPORTATION:

Plessy v. Ferguson—163 US 537 (1896): Supreme Court railway case that made "separate but equal" the law of the land for fifty-eight years.

> **Plaintiff:** Homer Plessy, a Black shoemaker whose challenge of the Louisiana Separate Car Law backfired when the Supreme Court sided with the Louisiana court in favor of segregation.

> **Finding and Effects:** The court found that separating Black and white train passengers was not a violation of

the Fourteenth Amendment's "equal protection" provision so long as the facilities for Black people were equivalent to those for whites. *Plessy*'s effect was to sanction all forms of segregation until the Supreme Court declared the doctrine of "separate but equal" unconstitutional in public education in *Brown v. Board of Education.*

Mitchell v. United States—313 US 80 (1941): Supreme Court railway case that found the railway company's eviction of Mitchell from an all-white Pullman car discriminatory but did not overturn the *Plessy* doctrine.

Plaintiff: Arthur Mitchell, a Black congressman who brought his challenge of segregated Pullman car accommodations to the Supreme Court after the Interstate Commerce Commission ruled against him.

Finding and Effects: The court ruled that under the Interstate Commerce Act and the Fourteenth Amendment, African Americans were entitled to "equality of treatment" on trains. But it stopped short of declaring segregation itself unconstitutional, and the ruling had little effect.

Morgan v. Virginia—328 US 373 (1946): Supreme Court bus ruling prohibiting states from imposing their segregation laws on interstate buses.

Plaintiff: Irene Morgan, a defense contractor employee whose challenge of a Virginia Jim Crow law on an

interstate bus was upheld by the Supreme Court on constitutional grounds.

Finding and Effects: The ruling said that when states
imposed their own Jim Crow laws on buses crossing state
lines, they violated the clause in the Constitution regulating commerce (the "commerce clause"). Southern bus
companies, claiming exemption from state laws as private businesses, dodged the ruling by putting their own
Jim Crow regulations in place until the *Keys* case (below)
prevented them from doing so.

Henderson v. United States et al.—339 US 816 (1950):
Supreme Court railway ruling that found dining-car segregation to be a violation of the Interstate Commerce Act.

Plaintiff: FEPC representative Elmer Henderson, who
brought his case to the Supreme Court after the Interstate
Commerce Commission ruled twice against him.

Finding and Effects: The justices condemned the
"artificiality of treatment" of the curtains separating
Black from white dining-car passengers as a violation
of the Interstate Commerce Act's ban on "undue and
unreasonable prejudice," but they failed to reconsider
Plessy.

Keys v. Carolina Coach Company—64 MCC 769 (1955):
Interstate Commerce Commission ruling that found

segregated seating on interstate buses a violation of the Interstate Commerce Act.

Petitioner: Army private Sarah Louise Keys, the first African American to bring a Jim Crow bus case before the ICC after she was forced to yield her seat on a North Carolina bus to a white marine.

Finding and Effects: The ICC's ban on Jim Crow bus seating on vehicles crossing state lines as "unjust discrimination and undue and unreasonable prejudice" under the Interstate Commerce Act was the only explicit repudiation of "separate but equal" in the area of interstate bus transportation by any court or administrative body. The 1955 ruling had little effect, however, until Attorney General Robert F. Kennedy pressed the ICC to enforce it during the 1961 Freedom Riders' campaign.

NOTE: The *Keys* case file was shredded by the National Archives when the ICC was abolished in 1995, along with all the other motor carrier cases the ICC heard. Limited documents on *Keys* are contained in the files of the Department of Justice. Dovey Roundtree's account is the only firsthand record of the history of this case.

NAACP v. St. Louis–San Francisco Railway Company—297 ICC 335 (1955): Railway companion case to *Keys v. Carolina Coach Company*.

Petitioner: The NAACP.

Finding and Effects: Finding identical to *Keys*, with little effect until Kennedy's intervention.

Gayle v. Browder—352 US 903 (1956): Supreme Court case that upheld Alabama federal court ruling declaring segregated bus travel within individual states unconstitutional.

Plaintiff: Montgomery, Alabama, mayor W. A. Gayle, who appealed the Alabama court's ruling in *Browder v. Gayle*, the case brought by Aurelia Browder and three other Black women after Rosa Parks's defiance of the city's Jim Crow bus law. NOTE: Parks was not a plaintiff in the case, but her actions triggered the Montgomery Bus Boycott, which vaulted the Reverend Martin Luther King Jr. to national prominence and birthed the civil rights movement.

Finding and Effects: The justices declared that segregated bus travel within individual states violated the Fourteenth Amendment. Although they did not explicitly overturn *Plessy*, as they had in *Brown v. Board of Education* two years earlier, their decision, in combination with the ICC's ruling in *Keys* and *NAACP* regarding travel across state lines, marked a major step forward in ending Jim Crow on vehicles within and among the states.

Boynton v. Virginia—304 US 454 (1960): Supreme Court case that found bus terminal segregation to be a violation of the Interstate Commerce Act and inspired the Freedom Rides.

Plaintiff: Howard University law student Bruce Boynton, who sued in Virginia court after being arrested for trespassing when he entered a whites-only restaurant in a Richmond bus terminal.

Finding and Effects: The ruling spelled out what the ICC's decision in *Keys* and *NAACP* had implied—that the Interstate Commerce Act's antidiscrimination protection covered not just the vehicles but the terminals servicing them as well. The major historical significance of *Boynton* was that it triggered the Freedom Rides, which prompted action by Attorney General Robert Kennedy to ensure that the ICC enforced its earlier rulings in *Keys* and *NAACP* as well as the Supreme Court's ruling in *Boynton*.

EDUCATION:

Gaines v. Canada—305 US 337 (1938): Supreme Court case that found Missouri's refusal to admit a Black student to the state's only law school a violation of the Fourteenth Amendment's "equal protection" guarantee.

Plaintiff: Lloyd Gaines, who sued in the state's supreme court upon being denied admission to the University of

Missouri Law School and told he must go outside the state for a legal education.

Finding and Effects: The court's ruling that a state must either provide Black students separate legal training equal to that of whites or admit them to the white law school marked a crucial first step in the legal assault on school segregation. The lawyers' campaign for enforcement of the ruling died with the mysterious disappearance of Gaines, but the case helped lay the foundation for *Brown*.

Sipuel v. Board of Regents of the University of Oklahoma— 332 US 631 (1948): Supreme Court case that ruled the state of Oklahoma must provide Black students with a law school education equivalent to that of whites but sent the matter of implementation back to the lower court.

Plaintiff: Ada Lois Sipuel, a minister's daughter, who sued after being first denied admission to the University of Oklahoma's all-white law school and then told to wait until there were enough Black applicants to justify building a separate law school.

Finding and Effects: The justices ruled initially in favor of Sipuel, but when the university roped off a section of its white law school for her and called it equal, the Supreme Court referred the matter back to the lower court, which supported the law school's separation policy. Thus the ruling had no effect.

Sweatt v. Painter—339 US 629 (1950): Supreme Court ruling that found separate law school facilities to be a violation of the Fourteenth Amendment's "equal protection" guarantee.

Plaintiff: Heman Marion Sweatt, a Texas mailman who sued the University of Texas when it denied him a spot in its law school and offered him three basement classrooms in an office building as an alternative venue for his law school education.

Finding and Effects: The justices ruled that the university must admit Sweatt to its law school since it could not provide equivalent legal education outside it. For the first time, the court recognized that separation in and of itself limited a person's educational opportunity, and it listed specific unacceptable differences in the Black and white law school facilities. Along with the *McLaurin* case (below), *Sweatt* set the stage for the all-out assault on *Plessy* in *Brown*.

McLaurin v. Oklahoma State Regents—339 US 637 (1950): Supreme Court ruling that found segregation in a state graduate program to be a violation of the Fourteenth Amendment's "equal protection" guarantee.

Plaintiff: George McLaurin, a Black doctoral student

who sued the University of Oklahoma when it forced him to sit in the hallway and then in a "Reserved for Colored" area of the main classroom.

Finding and Effects: The justices ruled that separating McLaurin from the other students prevented him from obtaining an education equivalent to theirs, and they required the university to treat McLaurin in the same way as the white students. Without overturning *Plessy,* the court acknowledged that separate could never be equal.

Brown v. Board of Education of Topeka, Kansas—347 US 483 (1954): Landmark Supreme Court decision that expressly overturned the "separate but equal" doctrine established by *Plessy v. Ferguson* (included *Briggs v. Elliott* [SC], *Davis v. County School Board of Prince Edward County* [VA], *Belton v. Gebhart* [DE], and *Bolling v. Sharpe* [DC]).

Plaintiff: Oliver Brown, father of Linda Brown, plus thirteen other parents in Topeka, Kansas, whose children were bused to all-Black schools instead of being admitted to white schools, and hundreds of other plaintiffs with similar segregation complaints.

Finding and Effects: In what is generally considered the most important ruling of the twentieth century, the Supreme Court struck down *Plessy* directly by stating that the doctrine of "separate but equal" had no place in

America because it violated the Fourteenth Amendment's "equal protection" provision (and in the Washington, DC, case, a violation of the Fifth Amendment's guarantee of "due process"). Although *Brown* dealt only with public schools, the ruling was cited in dozens of other cases involving transportation and public facilities, eventually bringing an end to segregation in all areas.

The court set no deadline for compliance but ruled the following year in a case called *Brown II* that the states must desegregate their public schools "with all deliberate speed." This vagueness enabled southern states to mount a movement of so-called massive resistance.

FURTHER READING

Arsenault, Raymond. *Freedom Riders: 1961 and the Struggle for Racial Justice* (Pivotal Moments in American History Series). New York: Oxford University Press, 2006.

Barnes, Catherine A. *Journey from Jim Crow: The Desegregation of Southern Transit*. New York: Columbia University Press, 1983.

Bell-Scott, Patricia. *The Firebrand and the First Lady: Portrait of a Friendship: Pauli Murray, Eleanor Roosevelt, and the Struggle for Social Justice*. New York: Alfred A. Knopf, 2016.

Du Bois, W. E. B. *The Souls of Black Folk*. (The Oxford W. E. B. Du Bois). Edited by Henry Louis Gates Jr. New York: Oxford University Press, 2007.

Escobar, Gabriel. "Saluting Military Pioneers, Past and Present: Former WAC Addresses Black Women's Convention." *Washington Post*, E1, December 8, 1997.

Fox, Margalit. "Dovey Johnson Roundtree, Barrier-Breaking Lawyer, Dies at 104." *New York Times*, A1, May 21, 2018.

Green, Constance McLaughlin. *The Secret City: A History of Race Relations in the Nation's Capital*. Princeton, NJ: Princeton University Press, 2015. Originally published 1967.

Janney, Peter. *Mary's Mosaic: The CIA Conspiracy to Murder John F. Kennedy, Mary Pinchot Meyer, and their Vision for World Peace*, 2nd ed. New York: Skyhorse Publishing, 2013.

Kersten, Andrew E. *A. Philip Randolph: A Life in the Vanguard* (The African American Experience Series). Lanham, MD: Rowman & Littlefield Publishers, 2006.

King, Martin Luther, Jr. *A Testament of Hope: Essential Writings and Speeches*. New York: Harper Reprint, 2003.

Kluger, Richard. *Simple Justice: The History of* Brown v. Board of Education *and Black America's Struggle for Equality*. New York: Vintage Books, 2004. Originally published 1976.

Luxenberg, Steve. *Separate: The Story of* Plessy v. Ferguson *and America's Journey from Slavery to Segregation*. New York: W. W. Norton, 2019.

McCabe, Katie. "Dovey Johnson Roundtree: A Legal Pioneer, Finally Getting Her Due." *Politico*, December 30, 2018.

McCabe, Katie. "She Had a Dream." *Washingtonian,*
  March 2002.

McCabe, Katie, and Stephanie Y. Evans. "The Life of
  Dovey Johnson Roundtree (1914–2018): A Centenarian
  Lesson in Social Justice and Regenerative Power." In
  *Black Women and Social Justice Education: Legacies
  and Lessons.* Albany, NY: SUNY Press, 2019.

McCluskey, Audrey Thomas, and Elaine M. Smith. *Mary
  McLeod Bethune: Building a Better World: Essays and
  Selected Documents.* Bloomington: Indiana University
  Press, 1999.

Murray, Pauli. *Pauli Murray: The Autobiography
  of a Black Activist, Feminist, Lawyer, Priest, and
  Poet.* Knoxville: University of Tennessee Press,
  1989. Originally titled *Song in a Weary Throat: An
  American Pilgrimage.*

Putney, Martha. *When the Nation Was in Need: Blacks
  in the Women's Army Corps during World War II.*
  Metuchen, NJ: Scarecrow Press, 1992.

Robertson, Ashley N. *Mary McLeod Bethune in Florida:
  Bringing Social Justice to the Sunshine State.* Charleston,
  SC: History Press, 2015.

Roundtree, Dovey Johnson, and Katie McCabe. Foreword
  by Tayari Jones. *Mighty Justice: My Life in Civil Rights.*
  New York: Algonquin Books, 2019.

Roundtree, Dovey Johnson, Papers, National Archives for

Black Women's History of the Mary McLeod Bethune National Historic Site, Museum Resource Center, Landover, MD. (Collection limited to Dovey Roundtree's military papers.)

Weinraub, Judith. "A Long Life of Sweet Justice: Dovey Roundtree, Attorney and Role Model." *Washington Post*, D1, February 4, 1995.

Woodward, C. Vann. *The Strange Career of Jim Crow*. New York: Oxford University Press, 2002. Commemorative edition.

PHOTO CREDITS

67: Anthony Potter Collection/Hulton Archive/Getty Images; **68:** Bettmann/Getty Images; **75:** Alfred Eisenstaedt/The LIFE Picture Collection via Getty Images; **80:** Los Angeles Examiner/USC Libraries/Corbis via Getty Images; **89:** Everett Collection Historical/Alamy Stock Photo; **93 (top and bottom):** Dovey Johnson Roundtree Educational Trust; **99:** Don Cravens/The LIFE Images Collection via Getty Images/Getty Images; **101:** Jack Delano/Library of Congress/Interim Archives/Getty Images; **110:** Bettmann/Getty Images; **111:** Bettmann/Getty Images; **120:** Dovey Johnson Roundtree Educational Trust; **126:** Underwood Archives/Getty Images; **131:** Declan Haun/Chicago History Museum/Getty Images; **133:** Dovey Johnson Roundtree Educational Trust; **135:** Robert L. Knudsen. White House Photographs. John F. Kennedy Presidential Library and Museum, Boston; **141:** Richard Darcey/The *Washington Post* via Getty Images; **146:** Bettmann/Getty Images; **157:** Lee Balterman/The LIFE Picture Collection via Getty Images; **159:** Dovey Johnson Roundtree Educational Trust; **160:** Dovey Johnson Roundtree Educational Trust; **162:** Dovey Johnson Roundtree Educational Trust; **164:** Dovey Johnson Roundtree Educational Trust; **172:** Courtesy of Nancy Ruth Pattersoniq

INDEX